Comparative
Cultural
Analysis

Comparative Cultural Analysis

An Introduction to Anthropology

Keith F. Otterbein
State University of New York at Buffalo

HOLT, RINEHART AND WINSTON, INC.
New York   Chicago   San Francisco   Atlanta
Dallas   Montreal   Toronto   London   Sydney

Copyright © 1972 by Holt, Rinehart and Winston, Inc.
All rights reserved
Library of Congress Catalog Card Number: 72–179545

ISBN: 0–03–084417–7

Printed in the United States of America
2 3 4 5 6   090   9 8 7 6 5 4 3 2 1

Preface

This textbook is based upon a teaching technique which I developed five years ago for use in an introductory cultural anthropology course. The technique consisted of reducing many of the important topics in anthropology to a set of questions which incorporated, as answers to the questions, many of the key concepts of the discipline. A data sheet listed twenty-five questions and the accompanying concepts. The sheet contained no definitions of the concepts, since these were provided through classroom lectures. The first week of the course (it was a six-week summer course) consisted of lectures in which I discussed the topics and defined the concepts. For the remainder of the course the students read four different ethnographies and, using copies of the data sheet, recorded passages which provided information on the twenty-five topics. They also tried to identify the concepts which correctly described the passages which they had recorded. Methodologically the concepts represented the culture traits, processes, or activities which were described in the ethnographies. Throughout most of the course the students and I discussed the reasons for classifying the different ethnographic statements as examples of the various concepts. Then during the last week of the course we recorded on a chart the concepts which pertained to each culture. We were thus able to compare our four cultures in terms of the twenty-five topics and to draw inferences as to what topics might be functionally related. That is, we attempted to make intelligent guesses as to what culture traits and processes are related in the real world. For example, population size might be related to the type of subsistence technology practiced. Specifically, it was found that a small population size was associated with a hunting and gathering technology, and a large population size was associated with agriculture.

Last summer I once again taught introductory cultural anthropology, using the technique as it is set forth in this textbook. The data sheet this time listed thirty-two questions. (At the end of this book are examples of this data sheet.) The topics discussed and the concepts defined during the first two weeks of the course were taken from the chapters and sections of this book. During the remaining weeks of the course the same procedures were followed which had been employed the first time that course was taught. Since developing this course, I have three times incorporated this technique into a graduate survey course in cultural anthropology. Graduate students read ethnographies of their own choosing and used the list for note taking. I strongly recommended to them that these sheets be used for permanent note taking. This spring I utilized the technique again in an undergraduate course in African ethnology. The technique has been a satisfactory teaching device, both at the undergraduate and graduate levels.

This technique was developed in response to what I believe is a major defect in most anthropology textbooks. The ethnographic examples used in the textbooks are drawn from a large number of cultures—seldom do more than several examples come from any one culture. Often the examples are either extreme, rare, or atypical cases. In response, many instructors of anthropology, including myself, have found it easier to teach using ethnographic case studies, such as those published by Holt, Rinehart and Winston, Inc., than using a standard textbook. This allows us to illustrate concepts with examples from a limited number of cultures and to devote our time to discussions of functional interrelationships between culture traits and processes within specific cultures. The reading of these case studies shows a student how the different aspects of a cultural system are interrelated in each of a small number of cultures. Thus emphasis is not placed upon atypical examples taken out of context. Nor is the student confused by dozens of exotic examples from dozens of cultures.

In a volume titled *The Teaching of Anthropology* (Mandelbaum, Lasker, and Albert 1963), David Mandelbaum has expressed a similiar viewpoint in this way (1963:52–53):

> Good ethnographic monographs . . . make fine reading for undergraduates. I have found it effective to have students read one or two brief monographs in the first few weeks of introductory cultural anthropology. Even in a few weeks they can acquire some of the leading concepts which they can apply to the data in the monographs. The analytic, problem-tackling, frontier-exploring qualities of anthropology can be brought in usefully in these early stages, so that the student is not simply reading about quaint customs and discovering that he too has customs and culture, but is also encouraged to set his mind to seeing some order, themes, and linkages within a culture.

Four pedagogical purposes are also served by developing the above technique into an introductory anthropology textbook: (1) The book provides a succinct list of the major topics and concepts in cultural anthropology. Thus it can be used as a reference or as a glossary of terms. (2) The book assists students in learning the fundamental concepts of cultural anthropology by requiring them to find examples in ethnographic case studies which correctly illustrate the concepts. Most instructors and most textbooks do this for the student; however, if the student is asked to do it for himself, the learning process becomes active rather than remaining passive. (3) By reading and rereading portions of the textbook and by applying the concepts, the students develop a "set" which will make ethnographically important facts (that is, the data pertaining to theoretically important topics) readily apparent while the case studies are being read. (4) The book furnishes a systematic outline which can be used to record ethnographic data. Once the descriptions found in a particular case study have been classified as to what concepts they illustrate, the completed outline can be used by students in reviewing for examinations. Once two or more outlines have been completed, the cultures which have been succinctly described can be compared. Such comparisons can be used by the instructor to demonstrate the possible existence of functional relationships between culture traits and processes, and the outlines can be used by students in doing research projects and in writing term papers.

Basically what this book does is to lay out systematically the important topics and key concepts of cultural anthropology. The topics and concepts are discussed in detail in the following chapters, and they are summarized on a data sheet at the end of this book. This set of concepts is fundamental to all research in anthropology. It is the conceptual order that, so to speak, underlies the anthropological subculture. Mastery of this order is a *sine qua non* for becoming a professional anthropologist. Thus it is necessary for students—both those wishing only an introductory knowledge of anthropology and those wishing to become competent professionals—to learn the important concepts of cultural anthropology. This book (and it is the only one of its kind) provides a technique which makes it possible for students in a classroom situation to simultaneously learn many key concepts while becoming familiar with a few of the cultures which have been studied by anthropologists. Students learn to analyze a cultural system, as presented in an ethnography, in the same manner that an ethnographer analyzes the way of life of the particular people among whom he is conducting fieldwork.

Williamsville, N.Y. K. F. O.
June 1971

Acknowledgments

I am indebted to several individuals who have assisted me at various stages in the preparation of this manuscript. My wife, Charlotte Swanson Otterbein, encouraged me to develop the teaching technique presented here into a book which could be used in introductory cultural anthropology courses. She provided critical comments at each stage of the writing. The distinction between economic relationships within the local group and between local groups is the contribution of Terrence A. Tatje (see "Local Economy" and "Economy of Culture" in Chapter 2). George and Louise Spindler critically reviewed the manuscript in its earliest stages. My wife and the editorial staff of Holt, Rinehart and Winston, Inc., have spent many hours editing the manuscript.

Contents

CHAPTER 1

Introduction

When I was an undergraduate I told my father that I wanted to become an anthropologist. He asked me what I was going to do with it. I knew that his question meant: How are you going to earn a living? But at that time I did not care if I ever earned a living. I told him that an anthropologist studies people. I then went on to say that I wanted to be a cultural anthropologist and that cultural anthropology is the study of the way different groups of people live. He looked puzzled, so I told him that I wanted to go to a tropical island and study the sex life of the natives. That ended the conversation. Several years later I did go to a tropical island. The study resulting from this trip is a detailed description of the way of life of the Negroes who live on Andros Island in the Bahamas, and focuses on courtship, marriage, and the family (Otterbein 1966).

This introductory chapter describes, in more precise terms than I told my father, what cultural anthroplogists study and how they conduct their research. A few basic concepts are defined, and instructions are provided for using this book.

Basic Concepts

The primary concept employed by anthropologists is *culture*. It is used in two senses. First, culture refers to the way of life of a particular group of people. It is everything that a group of people thinks, and says, and does, and makes. Culture is learned: it is transmitted from generation to generation. When anthropologists refer to the culture of a people, they are referring to a large and diverse number of topics which include technological pursuits, marriage customs, military practices, and religious beliefs.

All the topics discussed in the next four chapters, with the exception of physical environment, are aspects of the culture or way of life of a people. Second, if the article *a* precedes the term culture, it refers to the particular group of people themselves. If the term *culture* is used in the plural, it refers to different groups of people. Although there is not complete agreement among anthropologists, perhaps the most satisfactory criterion for distinguishing one group of people—one culture—from another is language. It is an appropriate criterion because not only is language an important aspect of culture, but it is also the major means by which culture is transmitted or taught to the young. If two groups of people speak different languages, they are different cultures. Languages are different if the speaker of one language cannot understand the speaker of the other language. (The criterion of language is difficult to apply in those few regions of the world where there are "linguistic continuums" or "language chains." For example, the German-Dutch dialects spoken along the Rhine River constitute a linguistic continuum. Naroll [1968:248–249] has proposed a technique for dividing these continuums into "chain links," each link of which can be considered a culture.) Anthropologists have no difficulty in shifting from one usage of the term *culture* to the other; in fact, they often speak of the culture of a culture. For example, it is as easy to speak of the culture of the Yąnomamö as it is to say that the Yąnomamö are a South American Indian culture. (The way of life of the Yąnomamö, a South American Indian tribe, and of another group of people, the Qemant, peasants of Ethiopia, will be used throughout this book to illustrate many aspects of culture.)

The use of the term *culture* to refer both to a group of people and to their way of life entered the vocabulary of anthropologists after 1900, due primarily to the efforts of Franz Boas and many of his students. Until his death in 1941, Boas was the major figure in American anthropology. Prior to 1900 the term culture was used in a different sense—it referred to the "progressive accumulation of the characteristic manifestations of human creativity: art, science, knowledge, refinement . . ." (Stocking 1966:870). Different groups of people could have a greater or a lesser amount of culture. Thus Edward B. Tylor, one of the founders of anthropology, could state in 1888 that "among peoples of low culture . . ." (this passage is quoted in its entirety in the section dealing with cousin marriage). Tylor's definition of culture (1958:1; orig. 1871) as "that complex whole which includes knowledge, belief, art, morals, law, custom, and any other capabilities and habits acquired by man as a member of society" is ambiguous since it does not state that culture is acquired by men as members of particular cultures, nor does it make explicit that only creative, rational capacities were considered culture at that time (Stocking 1966).

Since the days of Franz Boas, the concept of culture has undergone modification and elaboration. The major direction in which these changes have occurred is toward a position which views a culture as an entity composed, on one hand, of beliefs, symbols, and values (Geertz 1957), sets of standards for perceiving, believing, evaluating, and acting (Goodenough 1970), cultural traditions (Beals 1967), or jural rules (Leach 1961), and, on the other hand, of interactive behavior, social interaction, and social structure (Geertz 1957), a material-behavioral system of interacting people and things (Goodenough 1970), relationships between human beings (Beals 1967), or statistical norms (Leach 1961). Thus a culture is viewed as consisting of rules (that is, statements of ideal behavior) and behavior (whether the behavior corresponds to the rules or not). Some anthropologists speak of the rules as being culture per se and the behavior as forming a social system; then the entity composed of rules and behavior together is termed a society, a sociocultural system, or for short, a cultural system. This distinction is important, for its forces the anthropologist to take cognizance of the ideals which motivate people and at the same time to examine the frequency with which a people conform to the rules. Attention is paid to this distinction in this book, particularly in the chapter titled "Family and Kinship."

For convenience and because most anthropologists—in conversation at least—still employ the term culture in its two senses, the dual usage of Boas will be maintained throughout this book. Thus, the entire way of life of a group of people is referred to as their culture, while at the same time the group of people themselves is referred to as a culture. Moreover, although some anthropologists use the term *society* in referring to a particular culture, cultures such as the Yạnomamö will not be referred to as societies, nor will the term *societies* be used as synonymous with the plural form of culture—cultures.

Cultures can be viewed as systems composed of overlapping subsystems. Four subsystems are usually distinguished (Beals 1967:250–251): economic, social, political, and belief systems. An economic system consists of the means by which the physical environment is exploited technologically and the means by which the products of this endeavor are differentially allocated to the members of the culture. A social system is composed of the relationships between kinsmen and the groups formed by kinsmen. A political system consists of organizational units, their leaders, the relationships which leaders have with members of their units, and relationships between units. And finally, a belief system is composed of the knowledge which people have of the world around them and the practices and customs by which people utilize that knowledge. Each subsystem forms a system in the sense that it is not possible to understand any aspect of a subsystem without knowing something about the other aspects of that subsystem. For example, it is not possible to understand how products are differentially allocated until one knows how each product is produced, who produces it, how scarce it is, and what materials from the physical environment are utilized in its production. By the same token, each subsystem can only be completely understood when something is known about the other three subsystems. For example, are the products allocated to kinsmen, political leaders, or supernatural beings? For this reason the four subsystems are said to overlap and to form a single cultural system. Various aspects of each of these subsystems are described in each of the main chapters of this book. The economic system is described in a chapter titled "Technology and Economy," the social system in a chapter titled "Family and Kinship," the political system in a chapter titled "Polity and Warfare," and the belief system in a chapter titled "World View and Life Cycle." Each of these subsystems is a network of inter-related culture traits.

The culture of a people is composed of innumerable culture traits. Although the *culture trait* has been defined as the "smallest identifiable unit in a given culture" (Herskovits 1948:170), the term in actual practice is applied to any aspect of a people's way of life. It is used in such an all-encompassing sense that, for example, every house or domestic structure in a culture, the most frequently occurring type of house in a culture, and the rules or "blueprint" used to build this typical house can all be con-sidered culture traits. In other words, a culture trait is a catch-all term for any pursuit, custom, practice, or belief characteristic of a particular group of people. Hence, it is a useful term for referring to an aspect of a culture. Sometimes cultures are described or summarized by lists of culture traits. (In the Conclusion of this book, a list of thirty-two culture traits is used to summarize Yąnomamö culture and Qemant culture.) These lists of culture traits may be short, ten or twenty items, or they may be long— one list exceeds 2000 items (Herskovits 1948:169–182).

Some culture traits are considered to be more important than other culture traits because they have been shown by anthropologists to be related to other culture traits. The more culture traits a particular culture trait influences or is influenced by, the more important it is deemed to be. Since important culture traits are interrelated, in the sense of having a mutual influence upon each other, they form networks or systems. Four such systems, described above, are the economic, social, political, and belief systems. They can be thought of as subsystems since they overlap—some important culture traits are members of two or more subsystems—and form a single cultural system. Important culture traits and the subsystems in which they are usually found are described in the four main chapters of this book. For an anthropologist an adequate description of a people's culture is a report which describes the important culture traits—and their interrelationships—which are present in the culture. A major purpose of this book is to set forth in systematic fashion a series of concepts which describe or summarize the important culture traits of a particular culture.

Cultures are distributed spatially over the earth's surface. Usually a culture occupies a specific portion of this surface; its territory can be delineated on a map. (Occasionally, perhaps because of military conquest, two or more cultures will occupy the same territory.) The members of most cultures are to be found living as members of specific local groups (Linton 1936:209–230). A *local group* is a spatially distinguishable aggregate of people. It may be as small as a single family or as large as a city. Local groups within a culture can vary in size and number. A culture can be so small—in either territory or population size—that it contains only one local group, or it can be so large that it contains hundreds of local groups. Local groups can usually be delineated on a map, just as cultures can be. If a sufficiently detailed map is available (that is, a map which shows man-made structures), local groups can be delineated by drawing circles around clusters of structures. Cultures, in a similar fashion, can be delineated by drawing circles around the local groups of each culture. This technique is graphically illustrated in Figure 1. The term *local group* is not

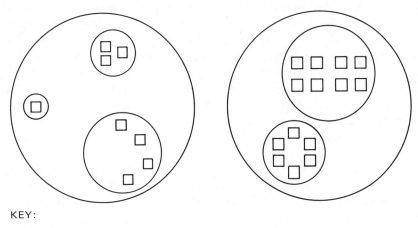

KEY:

Squares represent man-made structures
Small circles represent local groups
Large circles represent cultures

Figure 1.   Diagram of Basic Concepts—I

synonymous with the term *community*. For most anthropologists a community is "the maximal group of persons who normally reside together in face-to-face association" (Murdock *et al.* 1961:89). This definition has been understood to mean that when a local group becomes so large that each adult member does not know every other member of the local group, it ceases to be a community. Hence, large towns and cities—although local groups—are not communities in the sense that the term *community* is commonly used by anthropologists.

Anthropological Research

In order to learn about the way of life of a particular group of people, an anthropologist undertakes field research in that culture. Ideally this involves living with the members of the culture for a year or more and learning their language. A year of "fieldwork" is desirable in order that events which occur only once annually can be observed. A minimal facility in the language is necessary of course in order to talk with people. The time-honored method of conducting fieldwork is to take up residence with a local group. This may consist of living with a family, building a house, or pitching a tent. The location should be as advantageous as possible for watching daily activities. From this vantage point the anthropologist absorbs as much information as he can about the way the members of the local group live. He keeps a diary which describes both daily activities and special events. One of his first tasks is to map the location of important landmarks and houses. A census is also taken. The individuals from whom an anthropologist obtains his information are known as *informants*. The two major techniques of gathering information about a people's culture are observation and interviewing. These methods go hand in hand: the anthropologist asks his informants questions about a forthcoming event, he observes the event, and then he asks further questions concerning what he has observed. What he both sees and hears he records. Sometimes he is assisted by a camera and a tape recorder. Other more specialized techniques of data gathering may also be used. After gaining familiarity with the culture through his residence in one local group, the anthropologist may visit or change his residence to other local groups. However, an anthropologist usually spends most of his time studying the culture of a single local group.

Upon returning from "the field," the anthropologist begins the task of analyzing the massive amount of information which he has collected. This information is contained in his diary, in his maps, in his census reports, in his notes, in his photographs, and in his tape recordings. The first step in analysis is to index the diary and to tabulate the census data. The index, the census tables, and the other information collected are organized by topic. The topics may be ones developed for that particular culture, or they may be taken from a standard list. The list commonly used by American anthropologists is titled *Outline of Cultural Materials* (Murdock *et al.* 1961). This list is sometimes used to organize information as it is being collected in the field. The topics discussed in this textbook may also serve as a standard list. The next step consists of reading and rereading the information by topic. At this point the anthropologist begins to "see" the outline for his report coming into focus. The order of the topics may be changed. Eventually the list of topics becomes the outline for his report. The third step is to write the report, utilizing the information which has been organized by topic. The final product is a book which describes the culture of a particular group of people. Since the anthropologist is likely to have spent most of his time living with a single local group, the book is a description not of the lives of all members of the culture, but of the culture of a particular local group. Such a descriptive account is an *ethnography*. The book may also be referred to as an ethnographic monograph, and the information which it contains is known as ethnographic data. And not surprisingly, the anthropologist who conducted the field research and wrote the report is called an *ethnographer*.

Why do anthropologists go to all the trouble of doing fieldwork and writing ethnographies? There are, of course, personal reasons. The fledgling anthropologist may wish to get away from nagging parents, while the mature field researcher may wish to escape from academic pressures. Some anthropologists derive an immense thrill from visiting far-off, exotic places. Others are disenchanted with their own country. There are also various professional reasons for conducting field research. Each new description of a culture adds to the total number of cultures which have been adequately described by anthropologists. Much of what is known about the peoples of the world has been observed by and recorded by anthropologists in ethnographies. (I personally derive great satisfaction from realizing that in the twenty-first century, if someone wishes to know what life was like on Andros Island in the Bahamas 50 to 100 years before, there is only one source to which he can turn—my ethnography.) Each new monograph provides additional information to which fellow anthropologists may turn if they are conducting research that requires extensive ethnographic data from a large number of cultures. Another professional reason for doing fieldwork is to investigate a particular research problem. Such problems can range from the specific to the general. One anthropologist may wish to discover the effects of Westernization upon a particular culture; another may wish to use information about a particular culture to test a complicated theory of culture change.

In the writing of an ethnography, the anthropologist frequently employs concepts that represent the reality which he observed or had described to him by an informant. For example, an anthropologist observes that the members of the local group in which he is residing live in separate houses, each dwelling containing a married man and woman and their children. His census reports confirm this observation. Moreover, he learns that each adult has only one marriage partner and that newly-wed couples establish themselves in a dwelling separate from that of their parents. Because anthropologists refer to such family groups as "independent nuclear family households," this term is used in the ethnography. (The greater part of this book discusses the various concepts that have been utilized by anthropologists.) Each concept is a useful way of designating, in one to several words, a complex phenomenon—a culture trait—which might take several pages to describe. These concepts are often used at the ends of sections or chapters to summarize ethnographic data. In no instance should an ethnographer use the concepts as a substitute for a detailed description of the culture traits.

Once he has completed the ethnography, the anthropologist may choose to undertake comparative research rather than to initiate another ethnographic study. Comparative research may be undertaken for any one of several purposes. First, the anthropologist may compare his description of the culture he studied with descriptions of other cultures in order to derive new problems for research. For example, if a culture with a nomadic settlement pattern is contrasted with a culture which has year-round settlements, and it is noted that the former is a hunting and gathering people while the latter is an agricultural people, it can be inferred that the mode of subsistence is responsible for the type of settlement pattern. Moreover, the anthropologist may speculate that it is the sufficiency of food obtained or grown which is producing the greater permanence of settlements, since the local groups of the agricultural people do not have to move frequently to obtain enough to eat. Although there are no rules or special techniques for conducting comparative research of this type, usually the anthropologist compares cultures which are dissimilar and attempts to arrive at explanations for the cultural differences. Sometimes it is helpful for two anthropologists to work together in conducting the research. They may thus compare the cultures which each has studied.

Anthropologists may compare two or more cultures to simply discover similarities and differences; they may compare the same culture at two points in time in order to ascertain the amount of culture change which has occurred; they may compare a large number of cultures in order to determine the frequency with which different culture traits occur, either on a worldwide or regional basis; they may compare culture traits themselves in order to establish whether the traits cluster geographically. Underlying each of these endeavors, however, is usually the desire to explain cultural phenomena: Why the similarities and differences between cultures? Why does a culture change over time? Why are some culture traits common and others rare? Why are some culture traits found only in specific geographic regions? The tentative answers to these questions propose a relationship between two phenomena—either two culture traits or a culture trait and some other phenomenon, such as a geographic factor.

The most basic purpose for undertaking comparative research is to test proposed relationships between two phenomena—relationships proposed either from data in ethnographies or from comparative research. Different techniques have been devised for testing these proposed relationships, or hypotheses. One technique, known as the method of *controlled comparison*, consists of comparing two highly similar cultures. (This technique is described in the Conclusion of this book.) Another technique, which requires a sophisticated knowledge of research methodology and statistics, is known as the *cross-cultural survey* method. Usually as many as thirty different cultures, often more, are compared simultaneously. Research reports emanating from this method are known as *cross-cultural studies*.

How To Use This Book

This book is designed to be read in conjunction with several ethnographies. It presents a technique for simultaneously learning both the basic concepts of cultural anthropology and much of the important ethnographic information for several cultures. The technique is simple: one seeks in the ethnographies for examples of culture traits which correctly illustrate the concepts defined in the book. The concepts indicate what to "look" for in the ethnographies, and in finding appropriate ethnographic examples, one learns the definitions of the concepts. (A more detailed explanation of the rationale behind this technique is provided in the Preface.) The procedures set forth below describe how this technique can be employed.

The first step is to read this book. Each of the four main chapters is divided into sections; each section deals with a major topic in cultural anthropology. Each section builds upon previous sections; that is, concepts defined in one section are likely to be used in subsequent sections. Each section contains a question; the "answers" to the questions are concepts which have been defined in the sections. The questions are so phrased that they are inquiries about various aspects of the culture of a people. They are to be used as guides in discovering what culture traits are present and what culture traits are absent in a culture which is being studied. At the end of each section are two ethnographic examples which illustrate one or more of the concepts defined in the section. The examples are taken entirely from two ethnographies: (1) *Yąnomamö: The Fierce People* (1968) by Napoleon A. Chagnon. The Yąnomamö are a warlike tribe of South American Indians who inhabit the tropical forest region of southern Venezuela and northern Brazil. This ethnography was selected because it contains detailed information on nearly every topic discussed in this book, and it is one of the few reports of a culture which describes warfare that was actually occurring while the ethnographer conducted his fieldwork; (2) *The Qemant: A Pagan-Hebraic Peasantry of Ethiopia* (1969) by Frederick

C. Gamst. The Qemant are an agricultural peasantry who occupy a small segment of the mountainous Ethiopian Plateau. This monograph, like the Yąnomamö study, well describes most of the topics discussed in this book, and it provides an account of a culture which is politically absorbed into a modern nation. Thus the two peoples contrast greatly with each other. The questions used to elicit the ethnographic examples are listed on a form, labeled "data sheet," which appears at the end of this book. (Three blank data sheets are provided.) In order to place the ethnographic examples in their full cultural context, it is recommended that the Yąnomamö and the Qemant monographs be read in their entirety.

The next step is to read an ethnography other than the descriptions of the Yąnomamö and the Qemant, and to note the passages which illustrate concepts listed on the data sheet. Tentative decisions as to how to classify various culture traits should be made as the ethnography is read. Notes can be made in the margins of the ethnography and on a blank data sheet. On occasion it will be necessary to reread, and even to read a third time, sections which defined the concepts. When the reading of the ethnography is completed, a final decision as to what culture traits are present and what ones are absent must be made on the data sheet. The numbers preceeding the appropriate "answers" themselves can be underlined or circled. The basis for each decision should also be stated. It is also advisable to either paraphrase or quote relevant passages from the ethnography; page numbers should, of course, be given. Information to answer all questions with assurance is probably not available in the ethnography. When the analysis of the culture of a local group in terms of its culture traits is completed, one is ready to proceed to the analysis of another culture.

CHAPTER 2

Technology and Economy

Being human sets certain requirements which must be met if the members of a local group within a culture are to survive and reproduce. The physical environment must be capable of providing nourishment and, in other ways, supporting human life. Whether people can live in a particular region will depend upon the subsistence technology and the division of labor which they employ to exploit their environment. Exploiting the physical environment results in certain spacial consequences which are reflected in population density, settlement pattern, and settlement size. The products which are produced by the members of a local group are allocated differentially according to economic principles.

Physical Environment

Environmental location of a culture is one of the most important factors influencing the culture. The way of life of the members of a culture can be influenced by the opportunities which its environment presents, such as abundant animal life which may lead to a well-developed hunting technology, fertile soils which permit the development of horticulture and agriculture, and grasslands which provide excellent grazing grounds for herds of animals. Or the way of life can be influenced by the limitations which the environment presents, such as scarcity of animal life, cold temperatures which prohibit the growing of crops, and dry lands which provide little or no pasturage. This point of view, which looks upon the physical environment as providing both opportunities and limitations, is known as *environmental possibilism*. Although this approach has only recently come to be known by this phrase, environmental possibilism has

11

been accepted as a valid point of view by most anthropologists since the end of the nineteenth century. Anthropologists who subscribe to this position argue that the environment does not determine a people's way of life by forcing the members of every culture located in a particular type of environment to seek their livelihood in the same manner, but rather they argue that most environments provide several options or alternatives. For example, abundant wildlife, fertile soils, and grasslands may be available in a particular environment. Some cultures within the environment may utilize one or more of the options, and other cultures may utilize other options. Thus within this same environment some cultures may practice hunting and gathering, and other cultures may grow crops and graze animals (Vayda and Rappaport 1968:477–497; Sahlins 1964:132–147).

When anthropologists speak of a culture adapting to its environment, they mean that the culture has utilized one or more of the options available in the environment. Why a particular culture has selected certain options and not others is an important research problem for anyone attempting to understand that culture. Therefore, one of the first tasks confronting a person who is just beginning to read an ethnography is to note what type of physical environment the culture is located in and the options and opportunities available to the members of the culture.

Eight different types of physical environment can be distinguished. The description of the various environments, the limitations present, the opportunities available, and the location of the environments has been derived from Chapple and Coon's book *Principles of Anthropology* (1942: 73–95).

Deserts or dry lands are characterized by an annual rainfall of less than ten inches. The resulting dryness produces bare ground between plants. Extreme daily changes in temperatures prevail in most desert regions. The greatest limitation presented to the inhabitants of deserts is the scarcity of water. Root vegetables and animal life, both limited because of the water shortage, provide practically the only means of subsistence. Where oases are found or rivers flow through deserts, the possibility of agriculture exists. The five great desert areas of the world are North Africa and the Middle East, the Kalahari Desert of South Africa, central Australia, the North American Southwest, and the western coastal region of South America.

Tropical forests include both rain forests and semideciduous forests. Rain forests have heavy daily rainfall which results in dense vegetation. Temperatures remain high, approximately 80° Fahrenheit, throughout the year, with little daily variation. Semideciduous forests, although they can be classified as tropical forests, have a dry season in which many trees lose their leaves. Tropical forests provide only a few fruits and seeds, and there is little game to be hunted. Agriculture is difficult because soils are poor and clearings are hard to make and to keep weeded. The dense vegetation makes travel difficult except on rivers where canoe travel may be possible. The three major areas of tropical forest are the Amazon-Orinoco basin of South America, the Congo basin of Africa, and the forested regions of Southeast Asia and Indonesia.

Mediterranean scrub forests are characterized by mild, rainy winters and hot, dry summers. Vegetation consists of scrub forests of broadleaf evergreens and oaks. The forests provide abundant nuts and wild fruits. Small game is plentiful. Many different crops and fruits can be grown. The five main areas of Mediterranean scrub forests are the coastal regions of the Mediterranean Sea, the western coast of the United States, part of the coastal region of Chile, the tip of South Africa, and southwestern and southeastern Australia.

Temperate forests of broadleaf and coniferous trees obtain their growth from plentiful rain. These forests are further from the equator than either tropical forests or Mediterranean scrub forests. Great seasonal changes occur when these forest regions are located near the centers of continents. Animal life is moderately abundant, but there is little natural vegetable food. Soils are good and water is ample. Although hunting and agriculture are possible, cold winters make these modes of subsistence difficult. Any crops grown must be introduced from other environments. The three major regions of temperate forests are the eastern United States, most of Europe, and most of China.

Grasslands are characterized by rich subsoil, covered with grasses. One type of grassland, savanna, is dotted with trees, while another type of grassland, prairie and steppe, is usually treeless. There is great seasonal change in vegetation and foliage, and rivers crossing grasslands alternately flood and dry up. Grasslands usually support herds of large animals, such as antelope and buffalo, and they provide excellent pasturage for domestic animals. Savannas, in contrast to prairies and steppes with their thick sod, are easier to farm using simple farming implements. The six major grasslands are the midwestern region of the United States; the Ukraine region of Russia; the South American pampas of Argentina, Uruguay, and southern Brazil; the Brazilian highlands; central Africa north and south of the Congo basin; and northeastern Australia.

Boreal forests, consisting primarily of conifers, are cold, swampy tracts in which the temperature is usually below 50° Fahrenheit throughout the year and rainfall is slight. An abundant animal life flourishes, but agriculture is virtually impossible. Boreal forests extend in a belt around the northern hemisphere between 50° and 70° of latitude, including northern Canada, Scandinavia, and Siberia.

Polar lands include tundra, polar deserts (bare ground between patches of tundra), and permanent ice caps. Little snowfall and no forests, except for scrub vegetation and dwarf trees, characterize these lands. Animal life abounds, particularly fish and sea mammals. Hunting is the only type of subsistence possible. Polar lands fringe the border of the Arctic Ocean in North America, Europe, Asia, and the islands of the Polar Sea. The entire uninhabited continent of Antarctica is an ice cap.

Mountains, if they are located near the equator, may have all seven types of physical environments described above. What makes them interesting to anthropologists is that mountains in low latitudes have slopes and plateaus of moderate temperature and rainfall which are ideal for the development of intensive agriculture. In both the Old and the New World the domestication of many plants and animals occurred in mountain regions. The three great chains of mountains are the range which runs westward from Tibet to the Pyrenees, the chain which runs along the west coast of both North and South America, and the partially submerged chain which extends southeastward through the Malay Peninsula and out into the Pacific Ocean as far as New Zealand.

1. **In what type of physical environment is the culture located?**
   1. desert
   2. tropical forest
   3. Mediterranean scrub forest
   4. temperate forest
   5. grassland
   6. boreal forest
   7. polar land
   8. mountains

Most ethnographies either directly or indirectly describe the physical environment in which the culture is located. Since mountains may have other types of physical environment associated with them, it is possible to have more than one "answer" to this question—mountains and one or more other types of physical environment. In order to confirm one's judgment, the culture can be located on a climatic or environmental map in a standard world atlas.

———————

The Yąnomamö of southern Venezuela and northern Brazil live in a tropical forest region interspersed with mountains (Chagnon 1968:18):

The general area around Kąobawä's [the headman] village is a low, flat plain interrupted occasionally by gently rolling hills and, more rarely, by a few low mountain ridges. The land is entirely covered with jungle, even the tops of the mountain ridges.
The jungle is relatively dense and characterized by numerous species of palm and hardwood trees. The forest canopy keeps the sunlight from

penetrating to the ground, but scrub brush and vines manage to grow in relatively great abundance in most places, making it difficult to walk along the trails. Thorny brush is especially heavy along the banks of streams, where adequate sunlight and a constant supply of water provide ideal circumstances for its growth.

The Qemant live on the Ethiopian Plateau, a physical environment which can be classified as mountains (Gamst 1969:18):

Qemantland, a somewhat rugged part of the northwestern region of the plateau lying 18 miles to the north of Lake Tana, varies in altitude from 4000 to over 10,000 feet. Irregular in shape, it measures approximately 30 miles by 50 miles.

Photographs depict the mountainous terrain (Gamst 1969:21,27,80).

Several types of physical environments are associated with the plateau —desert, grassland, and temperate forest (Gamst 1969:20):

The ecological zones of the Qemant area are also found throughout much of the Ethiopian Plateau. These zones are best explained by the Ethiopians' own system of categorization as follows:
1. *Qolla.* Ranging from sea level to 7000 feet. Warm to hot climate; often disease ridden. Some parts are humid during the big rains. Characteristic crops are white *tef* (an important cereal with grains the size of fine sand and indigenous to northern and central Ethiopia), sorghums, cotton, and finger millet.
   a. *Baraha.* Lowest and hottest of the *qolla.* Said to have spontaneous grass and forest fires, and thought to be excessively unhealthy.
   b. *Medera bada* (land with nothing). Driest of the *qolla.* Refers to true desert, whereas *baraha* is semidesert.
2. *Wayna dega.* Ranging from 6000 to 9000 feet. Temperate climate. Characteristic crops are red *tef*, wheat, barley, and peas.
3. *Dega.* Ranging from 8000 to 15,000 feet. Cool to cold zone. Barley is the principal *dega* crop, but lentils, edible flax, and broad beans will also grow, although frost kills them in certain years. *Chowqe*, ranging from 12,000 to 15,000 feet, is the coldest and highest projections of the *dega.* Descriptive of the uninhabited higher mountain slopes, such as Ras Dajan and Guna. No farming and little grazing is done here.

Subsistence Technology

The various options within a physical environment lie dormant until they are exploited technologically by the members of a culture. Therefore, those options which will be utilized are determined by the subsistence technologies available to the people. Subsistence technologies are the activities which people perform to exploit their environment in order to gain a livelihood. In anthropological terms, the subsistence technologies utilized by a culture are the means by which that culture adapts to its physical environment. There are four basic subsistence technologies: hunting and gathering, animal husbandry, horticulture, and agriculture. Some cultures rely almost exclusively upon one of these basic technologies, while others rely upon a combination of two or more. Cultures which utilize two of the basic subsistence technologies are probably taking greater advantage of the options provided by the physical environment than are cultures which utilize only one subsistence technology (Bohannan 1963:212–216; Chapple and Coon 1942:142–197).

Hunting and gathering (including fishing) consists of techniques of obtaining natural foodstuffs—animal and vegetable—from the environment, using implements fashioned from materials obtained directly from the same source. Hunting, which is usually a male task, requires skill in the use of implements such as clubs, throwing sticks, bolas, spears, harpoons, spear throwers, bows and arrows, blowguns, slings, firearms, nets, snares, dead-falls, pitfalls, stakes, box traps, and spring traps. Hunters may work alone or in groups, depending upon whether the cooperation of several hunters is advantageous. Gathering, on the other hand, is usually performed by women and children. Often it requires less skill and fewer implements than hunting. Gatherers use knives, digging sticks, bags, baskets, wooden bowls, or other simple containers. Frequently they work together for companionship and for joint child tending. Fishing, a form of hunting, may be carried out by men, women, and children. Skill is required in the use of hooks and line, fish spears, bows and arrows, canoes, boats, dams, weirs, seine nets, casting nets, basketry traps, and fish poisons. Fishing may be done individually or in groups.

Animal husbandry is the practice of breeding and raising domesticated animals. Such animals require constant attention. Animals may be used for food, as a means of transportation, in hunting or herding other animals, and for their skins, hair, or feathers. The food use of animals includes not only meat, but also milk, eggs, and blood; the transportation use includes riding, packing, hauling, and plowing. Except for small animals which live near or within the family homestead, men and older boys usually tend animals.

Horticulture is the technology of farming or raising crops with the use of hand tools such as a digging stick or hoe. Fields or gardens are usually prepared by clearing the land of grass, bush, and trees. Often the vegetation removed from the land is heaped and burned, and the ash used to fertilize the soil. This is referred to in ethnographies as *slash-and-*

burn agriculture. The soil is prepared by being hoed or by being broken up with a digging stick. The types of crops planted, using this technique, include grains (such as Indian corn or maize, wheat, millet, and sorghum) and roots (such as manioc, cassava, yams, and potatoes). As the crops grow they are weeded, and when the plants are mature they are harvested. After two or three years the fertility of the fields has usually declined. They are allowed to return to fallow, either bush or jungle. New fields must then be cleared. Anthropologists call this practice *shifting cultivation.* Men usually do the difficult tasks of felling trees, cutting bush, and breaking up the soil, while women do the less strenuous tasks of planting, weeding, and harvesting.

Agriculture is the technology of farming with a plow and draft animal. This technique is confined to the Old World where the plow was invented. The use of the plow distinguishes agriculture from horticulture. Usually agriculture is a more intensive form of cultivation than horticulture. Fields are permanent and are kept fertilized with animal and human refuse. Grains, rather than root crops, are more likely to be planted. Men do the plowing and usually assist their wives in planting, weeding, and harvesting. Agriculture is a more efficient method of cultivation than horticulture because more crops can be raised per unit of land.

2. What subsistence technology is dominant (or codominant)?
    1. hunting and gathering
    2. animal husbandry
    3. horticulture
    4. agriculture

If the members of a culture gain their subsistence largely through one of the above technologies, that subsistence technology should be noted as being dominant. One may find that two technologies are approximately equal in importance in terms of the contribution which they make to the food supply. Importance can be measured either in terms of nutrient content in the diet or in terms of caloric intake. Although most ethnographies are silent on these two matters, it is probably easier to estimate caloric contribution to the diet. If two technologies appear to make approximately equal caloric contributions, then both should be recorded. The technologies are said to be codominant. Three such systems of codominance which the student should be on the lookout for include: (1) hunting and gathering/ horticulture, (2) animal husbandry/horticulture, and (3) animal husbandry/agriculture.

Horticulture is the dominant subsistence technology for the Yano-mamö (Chagnon 1968:33–36):

Although the Yạnomamö spend almost as much time hunting as they do gardening, the bulk of their diet comes from foods that are cultivated. Perhaps 85 percent or more of the diet consists of domesticated rather than wild foods—plantains are by far the most important food in the diet. . . .

The first operation in making a new garden is to cut the smaller trees and brush; the bigger trees, *kayaba hi*, are left standing until the under-brush is removed. Then the big trees are felled with axes and left lying on the ground to dry out in the sun. . . .

After the brush has dried out and the larger trees felled, the portable timber and brush is gathered up into piles and burned, each man having several fires going in his own patch, to which he hauls the brush as he gathers it up. Usually, the fires are built under or next to one of the larger logs. In this way the logs dry out even more completely and can be easily chopped up by the women for firewood. The ashes are not scattered to improve soil fertility. . . .

Each man's garden contains three or four varieties of both plantains and bananas. The larger portion of the cultivated land will contain plan-tains, as they produce a higher yield than bananas. The garden will also have a sizeable patch of sweet manioc, a root crop that is boiled or refined into a rough flour by grinding it on a rock and then converting the flour into thick, round cakes of baked cassava bread. . . .

Next in importance are three other root crops: taro, sweet potatoes, and mapuey. All of these resemble potatoes; they are usually boiled, but occasionally they are roasted directly over the coals. . . .

The dominant subsistence technology for the Qemant is agriculture (Gamst 1969:2):

The fertile soils of Qemantland support an economy based upon agri-cultural technology, including the plow, draft animals, and other live-stock which are secondary to the crops in the subsistence pattern. Cereals, legumes, oil seeds, and root crops are the staples of the economy, some being first domesticated as early as five thousand years ago by the ancestors of the Qemant.

Population Density

The population density of a culture is strongly influenced by the adaptation which the culture has made to its environment. Since the cul-tures within a particular environment utilize the different options provided by the environment in different ways, the population density of the cultures will vary depending upon their mode of adaptation. Thus it is not possible to predict accurately the population density of a culture simply from a knowledge of the type of physical environment in which the culture is located, although Mediterranean scrub forests, temperate forests, grasslands, and some mountains are more suited to human habitation than are deserts, tropical forests, boreal forests, and polar lands. Since the various types of subsistence technologies provide for different modes of adaptation, it is to be expected that the population density of a particular culture will depend to a large extent upon the type of subsistence technology practiced by the members of the culture. Of the four basic types of subsistence technology, agriculture can support the most dense population and hunting and gathering the least dense population. Animal husbandry and horticulture, in terms of the density of population which they can support, occupy an intermediate position between agriculture and hunting and gathering. Hence, population density varies with the manner in which a culture adapts to its environment, as mediated by the type of subsistence technology practiced.

3. What is the population density of the culture?

If the population density figure for the culture is not given in the ethnography, it can be computed by dividing the number of square miles occupied by members of the culture into the population size of the culture. The formula is as follows:

$$\text{Population Density} = \frac{\text{Population Size}}{\text{Square Miles}}$$

The resulting figure will give the population density in terms of the number of persons per square mile. Usually the population size of the culture is presented in the introductory section of the ethnography. Since some ethnographies give the population size at different time periods, the student should note which time period his data pertain to. If the population size is not given, the calculation cannot be performed. (However, if the population density is given, the population size can be computed by multiplying the number of persons per square mile by the number of square miles.) Sometimes the number of square miles occupied by members of the culture is presented and sometimes not. If it is not given, it usually can be computed by estimating from a map which shows the territorial boundaries of the culture. Most ethnographies provide the reader with such a map. The estimate can be performed by multiplying the approximate east-west dimension of the culture by the approximate north-south dimension, and subtracting any areas within this rectangle which are not occupied by the culture. Since it is necessary that the figure for the number of square miles pertain to the same time period as the population size figure in order for the calculation to be correctly computed, special attention should be paid to the time period to which the map applies.

The ethnographer estimates that "in total numbers their population [Yąnomamö] probably approaches 10,000 people, but this is merely a guess" (Chagnon 1968:1). He also provides a frontispiece map, p. iv, which shows the location of the Yąnomamö. The scale for the map is given in kilometers (1 kilometer = .62 miles); therefore, the scale must be converted to miles. Estimating from the map, Yąnomamö territory is approximately 200 miles by 200 miles, or roughly 40,000 square miles. Using the formula one can compute the population density at .25 persons per square mile.

Gamst estimates the population of the Qemant between 20,000 and 25,000 (1969:1). In another place (see Question 1) he describes their territory as measuring 30 miles by 50 miles—in other words, 1,500 square miles. Utilization of the formula yields a population density of approximately 15 persons per square mile.

Subsistence Participation

Whether men or women play the dominant role in subsistence pursuits has an important influence on several aspects of the family and kinship. If men play the major role, it is to be expected that men will own the property—tools, animals, and land—used in subsistence, that related men will live together and bring their wives to live with them, and that men will form the core membership of kinship groups. If women play the major role, it is to be expected that women will own the property used in subsistence, that related women will reside together and their husbands will come and live with them, and that women will form the core membership of kinship groups (Murdock 1949:36–39,201–218). These several aspects will be discussed in the next chapter.

On the other hand, the basic subsistence technology of a culture is an important factor influencing which sex will play the dominant role in subsistence pursuits. Since men are physically stronger than women, difficult technological activities fall to men and less strenuous pursuits fall to women. Thus hunting, animal husbandry, cutting bush, and plowing—being difficult tasks—are usually male activities, while gathering, planting, weeding, and harvesting—being less difficult tasks—are usually female activities. As was pointed out above in the "Subsistence Technology" section on p. 16, hunting is usually a male activity and gathering a female activity, while fishing may be carried out by both men and women. Animal husbandry is primarily a male occupation. Since agriculture usually requires more difficult tasks than horticulture (remember that draft animals

require constant attention), women are likely to participate more in horticulture while men are likely to participate more in agriculture. None of the
relationships suggested above, between the type of technology and who
plays the dominant role in the activity, necessarily holds for every culture.
Therefore, whether men or women participate more in subsistence pursuits
must be empirically investigated for every culture which is being studied,
either by an ethnographer in the field or by a scholar undertaking an
analysis of the published literature on the culture.

4. **Who plays the major role in the dominant (or codominant) subsistence
   technology?**
   1. males predominate
   2. females predominate
   3. equal participation by both sexes
   4. specialists

If men contribute more time to the dominant subsistence technology
than do women, it should be noted that "males predominate," and if women
contribute more time than do men, it should be noted that "females
predominate." If both sexes contribute roughly the same amount of time
to the dominant subsistence technology practiced by the members of the
culture, "equal participation" should be designated. Although cases are
apparently rare, it should be noted if there are "specialists," rather than all
able-bodied men or women, who perform the major role in the dominant
subsistence technology. Specialists are individuals who have skills that all
members of the culture do not possess. Specialists employ these skills, either
part time or full time, to earn their own livelihood, either by selling or
trading their skills or the products of their labors. If there are codominant
subsistence technologies (see "Subsistence Technology" on p. 17), it is
possible that males will predominate in one technology and females will
predominate in the other. Which sex predominates for each technology
should be recorded.

———————

Chagnon provides a clear statement that men play the dominant role
in Yąnomamö horticulture (1968:90):

Within an hour after it is light the men are in their gardens clearing
brush, felling large trees, transplanting plantain cuttings, burning off
dead timber, or planting new crops of cotton, maize, sweet potatoes,
yuca, taro, or the like, depending on the season. They work until
10:30 A.M., retiring because it is too humid and hot by that time to
continue with their strenuous work. Most of them bathe in the stream
before returning to their hammocks for a rest and a meal.
    The women usually accompany their husbands to the garden and

occupy themselves by collecting firewood or helping with planting and weeding.

Males play the major role in Qemant agriculture, according to Gamst (1969:79):

> Like other Qemant men, Erada and his sons prepare the fields for planting, using a wooden scratch plow, with an iron-shod tip, which is pulled by two oxen. . . .
> . . . The men and boys, sometimes aided by women and girls, sow grains, pulses, and oil seeds by the broadcast method and plant potatoes, cucurbits, garlic, and shallots in the ground by hand. Fields are replowed to cover the seeds. . . .
> All males and females in Erada's family weed fields with an iron-bladed hoe or with their hands. . . .
> Harvesting of cereals, oil seeds, and pulses is usually done by males, but females help when needed. . . . Threshing is done by males on a circular threshing floor. . . .

Division of Labor

The division of labor in a culture is based upon the allocation of tasks. In all cultures different tasks are allocated to different individuals on the basis of sex, age, and sometimes specialized training. The division of labor by sex is universal; as pointed out in the previous section, the greater strength of men makes them more suitable than women for carrying out difficult technological activities. Thus men hunt, raise animals, cut bush, and plow, while women gather, plant, weed, and harvest. Women are also responsible for the rearing of children, since they are the ones who bear children and nurse them. The division of labor by age is also universal; the human infant matures slowly over a long period (approximately fifteen to twenty years) in which it is dependent upon its parents. Therefore, the activities of a child differ from those of an adult. As a person grows old and his faculties deteriorate, he can no longer perform the tasks which adults in his culture normally perform. Hence, all cultures recognize at least three stages in a person's life: childhood, adulthood, and old age. There is no culture known to anthropologists which does not have a division of labor which is based upon at least the two criteria of age and sex.

In some cultures a third criteria—specialized training in different techniques—is found. In these cultures individuals, usually men, specialize in performing different tasks. They may perform the tasks as a part of a joint productive effort, or an individual alone may perform a task which results in a single product, such as a pot, a rug, a canoe, or a basket. These products or the performance of the techniques used to produce the products are either sold or traded to other members of the culture for goods and services. If these specialists devote only a part of their time, either daily or seasonally, to their tasks, they can be classified as *part-time specialists*. If they devote all of their time to their tasks, they can be classified as *full-time specialists*. A culture, of course, can have both part-time and full-time specialists (Chapple and Coon 1942:250–256).

Anthropologists and sociologists both have been interested in the division of labor because of its relationship to the growth and development of cultures. It is in the simplest of cultures that one finds a division of labor based upon age and sex only. In the most complex cultures, such as the industrial nations which now dominate the earth, the division of labor is based upon full-time specialists. In other words, as cultures grow in size and complexity their division of labor changes from being based on age and sex to being based on full-time specialists. This increase in the degree of specialization is seen as being both a result of and a cause of the development of particular cultures.

5. What is the division of labor?
   1. age and sex only
   2. part-time specialists
   3. full-time specialists

If there are no specialists, either part-time or full-time, in the culture, then the division of labor will be based upon age and sex only. On the other hand, if there are specialists in the culture, then the division of labor cannot be based upon age and sex only. Since both part-time and full-time specialists can be present in the same culture, it is best to list every specialist and then to make a decision as to whether he is part-time or full-time. If both types of specialists are present, both categories should be recorded. Simple counting will provide the ratio between the number of part-time and full-time specialists.

The Yąnomamö have part-time specialists who prepare items for intervillage trade (see Question 9). Two of the major items produced for trade are hammocks manufactured from cotton and clay pots (Chagnon 1968:100–101).

The Qemant have both part-time and full-time specialists. Part-time specialists include "local feudal officials" and carpenters, while full-time specialists include the *wambar*, "a full-time politicoreligious specialist," and itinerant traders (Gamst 1969:79,81,83).

Settlement Pattern

The physical distribution of the members of a culture within its territorial boundaries constitutes its settlement pattern. All peoples reside in local groups of various sizes, from small families to large cities. At any particular point in time each local group has a particular geographical location. Some local groups remain permanently at one location, while others move seasonally. Settlement patterns can be classified according to the size and spacial distribution of the local groups within the culture.

If the members of the culture are grouped into bands of approximately twenty to sixty individuals which shift from one section of their territory to another throughout the year, the culture can be categorized as having a *nomadic* settlement pattern. Whether individual bands own sections of the territory or not is an empirical problem which must be investigated for each culture. For many nomadic peoples the bands move within a prescribed annual cycle; that is, every year at the same time they return to the same section of their culture's territory. Other nomadic peoples have large bands which break up into smaller bands for several months out of the year. The members of some cultures spend part of the year, often winter, in permanent settlements and the remainder of the year migrating as bands. Such a settlement pattern is known as *seminomadic*.

Many cultures have settlement patterns in which the local groups remain at relatively permanent locations. Natural catastrophy, warfare, or depleted soils may on occasion force local groups to move, but once moved the settlements again become stable and take on the characteristics typical of the previous settlements. Neighborhoods of *dispersed homesteads* characterize some cultures whose technology is horticulture. Fields lie between the homesteads, which may be from several hundred feet to several hundred yards from each other. Thus neighborhoods are spread over several square miles. In contrast to neighborhoods of scattered homesteads are settlements of homesteads or houses which are close to each other. The local groups are *hamlets* or *compact villages*, which often have a social, economic, and ceremonial center. A market or a village square may serve these functions. The reason for distinguishing between hamlets and villages is that in some cultures there are compact villages with outlying satellite hamlets. Thus the settlement pattern is based upon both hamlets and compact villages. In terms of population size, any settlement under 5000 persons can be considered a hamlet or compact village. Settlements of over 5000 persons can be considered *towns* or *cities*. Although the figure of 5000 persons is arbitrary, it is an attempt to quantitatively distinguish between settlements which have primarily a local character and those that are urban and serve the needs of all the members of the culture and in some cases also individuals from other cultures. Towns and cities have a cosmopolitan character. Artisans, traders, and merchants gather in number. Since most urban dwellers do not know each other, administrative offices are needed to regulate the relationships between persons. A distinction is made between towns and cities because in some cultures there are cities with outlying satellite towns. Thus the settlement pattern is based upon both towns and cities.

The settlement pattern of a culture is influenced by a number of factors, several of which have already been discussed. The physical environment, the subsistence technology, the population density, and the division of labor all play a role in determining the size and spacial distribution of local groups. Hunting and gathering and animal husbandry both predispose a culture to being nomadic or seminomadic. Horticulture and agriculture, on the other hand, favor the more stable settlement patterns of dispersed homesteads, hamlets, and villages. If there is a high population density and the division of labor is based on specialists, towns and cities are likely. Warfare may also affect the settlement pattern by causing the members of the culture to live in fortified villages, towns, and cities, rather than dispersed homesteads.

6. What is the settlement pattern?
   1. nomadic
   2. seminomadic
   3. dispersed homesteads
   4. hamlets and/or compact villages
   5. towns and/or cities

Most ethnographies indirectly describe the settlement pattern of the culture. It should be noted whether combinations of hamlets and villages or towns and cities occur.

The Yąnomamö live in compact villages (Chagnon 1968:88–89):

Kąobawä's village is oval-shaped. His house is located among those of his agnatic kinsmen; they occupy a continuous arc along one side of the village. Each of the men built his own section of the village, but in such a way that the roofs coincided and could be attached by simply extending the thatching. When completed, the village looked like a continuous, oval-shaped lean-to because of the way in which the roofs of the discrete houses were attached. Each house, however, is owned by the family that built it.

Furthermore, an aerial picture and a drawing of a compact village are to be found in Chagnon's monograph (1968:19,27).

The settlement pattern of the Qemant is based upon dispersed homesteads (Gamst 1969:1,22):

Qemantland does not have compact villages. Instead, one to four wattle-and-daub walled houses topped by peaked thatch roofs constitute semi-isolated homesteads that are scattered across pastures and cultivated fields throughout the length and breadth of the land. Anywhere from one to four hundred of these homesteads are united socially to form a widely dispersed community.

As previously mentioned all Qemant live in dispersed settlements, and the Qemant of Karkar and Shelga are no exception. Homesteads consisting of single houses or clusters of two to four houses are located anywhere from 300 to 3000 feet from other homesteads. Clusters of ten to twenty houses are rare among the Qemant, and villages . . . do not exist.

Settlement Size

A complete picture of the settlement pattern is not available until the population of the largest settlement is known. This figure provides more information about a culture than does that of the average settlement size. Naroll (1956:693) has argued:

> To know the size of the largest settlement is usually to know the size of the largest and most diverse collection of specialists, and very often the size of the center of political and economic organization also. Here is usually the largest center of information. In a crude sense—although we cannot press the analogy too far—the largest settlement is the brain of the ethnic unit.

Having available information on the size of the largest settlement not only makes it possible to differentiate between villages (under 5000 persons) and towns (over 5000 persons), but it gives a measure of the degree of urbanization or cosmopolitanism of the largest settlement. In other words, the greater the population the greater the degree of urbanization. If the population of the largest settlement is, say, over 50,000 persons, we have evidence of a large urban concentration of people. On the other hand, knowing the largest settlement size provides an indication of what the maximum possible size of a nomadic band in that culture can be. It also provides the size of the permanent settlements when the settlement pattern is seminomadic and the size of the largest neighborhoods of dispersed homesteads when the settlement pattern is dispersed homesteads.

7. What is the population of the largest settlement?

It is not always easy to obtain this information directly from the ethnography. If census data for several local groups are given, then the population of the largest of these local groups should be listed. Often, however, the ethnographer simply states vaguely that settlements range in size, say, from 50 to 100 persons. When this is done, the maximal figure—in this case 100—should be noted. Sometimes it is simply necessary to guess, or approximation techniques can be used: (1) multiplying the number of homesteads in a large local group by the average number of persons in a household; (2) dividing the number of settlements into the total population.

The ethnography dealing with the Yanomamö provides both a table showing the size of selected villages and a statement of the range in settlement size. The size of the largest village in the table is 232 (Chagnon 1968:74). The maximal figure for the range is 250 (Chagnon 1968:1):

Some 125 widely scattered villages have populations ranging from 40 to 250 inhabitants, with 75 to 80 people the most usual number.

Since the figure of 250 is close to the figure of 232 and is Chagnon's approximation for the maximum village size, 250 should be listed as the population of the largest settlement.

An important Qemant community is Karkar, "until recently the chief religious center of the Qemant" (Gamst 1969:ix). Although not explicitly stated to be the largest settlement, its importance and size leaves little doubt that it is the largest Qemant community (Gamst 1969: 22–23):

A detailed study was made of the community of Karkar, which is divided into three subcommunities by a range of hills and an escarpment. One of these three segments, called Karkar Anchaw Mikael, was the actual site of the fieldwork. . . . The population of this segment in 1965 was 650, while the population of "greater" Karkar was 2640.

Thus the population of the largest settlement is 2640.

Local Economy

Economics deals with the allocation of goods and services, whereas technology deals with the production of goods and food supplies. In studying an economy one is interested in the manner in which goods and services are transferred from one party or group to another. The exchange and movement of goods and services can either be within the local group or between different local groups within the culture. In this section the allocation of goods and services within the local group will be considered. Anthropologists are indebted to Karl Polanyi, an economic historian, for identifying three different modes of allocation or principles of exchange, or as Polanyi called them, "forms of integration": reciprocity, redistribution, and market exchange (Polanyi 1957). Every economy is characterized by at least one of these principles. Many economies are based on two or all three of these principles; usually one principle will be dominant.

Reciprocity is the exchange of goods and services between units of the same kind, such as individuals, households, kinship groups, or local groups. Such exchanges usually occur between units which are already linked by social and ceremonial obligations; thus, reciprocity follows rather than creates such relationships. Reciprocity often takes the form of gift exchange since the distribution of goods of material value is not usually the purpose of reciprocity. The main reason for exchanges of this type is the maintenance of the obligations which exist between the units. Two types of reciprocity can be distinguished.

Balanced reciprocity is direct exchange in which goods and services of commensurate worth are traded within a finite period. That is, one unit in the exchange gives the other unit a gift; the gift must be "repaid" by a gift of comparable value, probably within a period of one year. There cannot be a one-way flow of goods—if the gift returned is of significantly less value or if it is not returned within the appropriate period of time, the social relationship upon which the exchange is based is disrupted. Thus balanced reciprocity is a way of maintaining relationships between units. (When reciprocity between local groups occurs, it is likely to be balanced reciprocity, and the members of the local groups carrying out the exchanges are likely to be nonkinsmen.)

Generalized reciprocity, on the other hand, is exchange in which goods and services flow predominantly one-way, with appreciation and respect flowing from the recipient. That is, one unit gives a gift; the gift need not be repaid within a finite period, and if it is repaid, the gift returned need not be of commensurate worth. Appreciation and respect, and sometimes deference, however, must be shown to the donor. Generalized reciprocity frequently occurs between close kinsmen who are members of the same local group. The sharing of large game animals which is common in hunting and gathering cultures and the distribution of meat from large domestic animals which sometimes occurs in cultures that practice animal husbandry, horticulture, or ariculture is a form of generalized reciprocity. The hunter or owner of the slaughtered animal receives prestige in exchange for his ability or generosity (Sahlins 1965).

Redistribution is the systematic movement of goods and services toward an administrative center and their reallocation by the authorities. Redistribution may be voluntary on the part of the members of the culture or it may be involuntary in that the administrative center uses agents to force the members to contribute goods and services to the authorities. The goods may be used to support the needy, to reward followers, to support armies, or simply to ensure the comfort of the authorities. The redistributive center can vary from the head of a band to the ruler of a large kingdom.

Market exchange is the exchange of goods and services according to the law of supply and demand. In market exchange, goods and services have a value or price which is established by supply and demand. General purpose money makes this possible, while authorities are necessary to enforce financial commitments. General purpose money, by definition, provides a medium of exchange, a standard of value, and a means of discharging obligations. Limited purpose money, on the other hand, serves only one or two of these functions. Both general purpose money and enforceable contract law need to be present for market exchange to operate efficiently. Marketplaces may or may not be present. The mere fact that markets occur is not evidence that market exchange is present. And by the same token, market exchange can occur without market sites being a part of the culture.

One or more of these three principles of exchange may be found within any local group. That principle which transfers the greatest number of goods and services from one party or group to another within a local group can be considered dominant. Usually redistribution will be more dominant than reciprocity, while market exchange will be more dominant than redistribution. Nevertheless, which principle of exchange is dominant in the local group must be ascertained through empirical investigation.

8. **Which principle of exchange is dominant in the local group?**
    1. balanced reciprocity between households
    2. generalized reciprocity between households
    3. redistribution through a local allocative agency
    4. market exchange

If households or homesteads exchange goods and services, including gifts, and redistribution and market exchange do not or only rarely occur, then reciprocity between households is the dominant principle of exchange in the local group. If there is a two-way flow of goods and services, the reciprocity is balanced; if the flow is one-way, the reciprocity is generalized. If there is an agency, such as the leader of the settlement or a religious official, who receives services and goods which are reallocated to persons within the local group, and this is the dominant principle of exchange, then it should be noted that redistribution through a local allocative agency occurs. In some instances it may be difficult to distinguish between redistribution and generalized reciprocity, since with both these principles of exchange there is a one-way flow of goods and services. They can, however, be differentiated: almost invariably the recipient in redistribution is a leader with high standing in the local group, whereas the recipient in generalized reciprocity is likely to be a person of low standing, perhaps a child (Sahlins 1965:163–164). If general purpose money is present and the law of supply and demand operates, then market exchange is dominant.

Both generalized and balanced reciprocity between households occur among the Yąnomamö. Generalized reciprocity occurs in the following situations (Chagnon 1968:33,91):

> On other [hunting] trips, we often managed to collect enough game in one day to feed the entire village.
>
> It is a happy occasion when one of the hunters bags a tapir, for everyone gets a large share of it.

On the other hand, balanced reciprocity also occurs (Chagnon 1968:7):

> Nor could I enter into their system of reciprocities with respect to food; every time one of them gave me something "freely," he would dog me for months to pay him back, not with food, but with steel tools. Thus, if I accepted a plantain from someone in a different village while I was on a visit, he would most likely visit me in the future and demand a machete as payment for the time that he "fed" me. I usually reacted to these kinds of demands by giving a banana, the customary reciprocity in their culture—food for food—but this would be a disappointment for the individual who had visions of that single plantain growing into a machete over time.

Moreover, a man who has married into the village hunts for his wife and her parents, and in turn he is provided with plantains by his in-laws (Chagnon 1968:91,93). Since the man has probably established his own household, balanced reciprocity between households occurs in this situation.

Although it is difficult to reach a decision as to which principle of exchange is dominant, the entire tenor of Yąnomamö culture leads one to infer that nothing is ever given without an expectation of a return. Therefore, it can be concluded that balanced reciprocity between households is the dominant principle of exchange in the local group.

Market exchange is dominant in Qemantland, both within the local group and between local groups. Gamst states (1969:81–83):

> The Qemant have at least four modes of distributing their production. Allocation of goods and services may be by formal market exchange inside of a marketplace, by informal market exchange outside of a

marketplace, by collection and redistribution in connection with ritual, and by reciprocity. . . .

Means of transportation and communication in the Qemant region are poorly developed, and the Qemant peasant has access only to his own regional marketing system, which is little affected by conditions outside Qemant society. Marketing, formal and informal, is the exchange of goods and services at prices arrived at by supply and demand.

Money is almost always used in formal marketing and is sometimes employed in informal marketing. Today the official Ethiopian copper and paper currency is used as the principal medium of exchange. . . .

Formal marketing is held at fixed times in marketplaces, usually little more than vacant clearings when the market is not being held. . . .

For the Qemant peasant, trading at a marketplace is a means of exchanging a commodity of which he has a slight surplus for another commodity which he lacks. . . .

In the marketplace, one might additionally . . . hear the latest of the customary pronouncements from the local feudal officials. These officials have long guaranteed the peaceful existence of the marketplace so that their region will prosper, and produce taxes, through trade and commercial traffic to centers of trade. . . .

Informal marketing consists of exchange between two persons in which middlemen are not involved, and money is seldom used. This trade may be transacted anywhere in a community at almost any time. In most transactions, a certain amount of one commodity is deemed equal in value to a certain amount of another commodity and the two are exchanged. Before livestock is exchanged, however, the price of the beasts is agreed upon in Maria Theresa dollars. If one of the parties in the transaction receives an animal worth less than the one he has given, he receives additional produce priced at the number of Maria Theresas needed to balance the exchange.

It appears from the above description that "formal marketing" occurs between local groups and that "informal marketing" prevails within local groups.

Both types of reciprocity also occur within local groups. Balanced reciprocity is described in the first paragraph below, and generalized reciprocity is described in the second paragraph (Gamst 1969:84):

Qemant distribute a significant part of their goods and services through modes of reciprocity. It may be a bond of reciprocity between breast father and breast child, between a man and his fictive mize brothers, among all members of a community mahebar association, or simply between two neighbors, interacting in a very limited context, who help one another with house repairs.

The items involved in reciprocal exchange are not easily equated. For example, a priest may use his influence on behalf of and give special blessings to a peasant who regularly feeds and occasionally labors for the priest. Two families might engage in a continuous round of giving gifts, including meals, to one another. A rich man may build up his social credit in the community by feeding and entertaining people and by giving rather generous compensation to those who occasionally till his fields for him.

Economy of Culture

The three different modes of allocation which may be found in local groups are also characteristic of entire cultures. The various local groups within a culture may be economically integrated through one or more of the principles of exchange. If they are not integrated, then there is no patterned exchange of goods and services between local groups. There may, however, be reciprocity between local groups; there may be redistribution through a nonlocal allocative agency such as an administrative center headed by a chief or king; or there may be market exchange.

The economic integration of cultures has received recent theoretical discussion by Elman Service (1962). In his book *Primitive Social Organization: An Evolutionary Perspective*, he has employed three different types of integration—social, political, and economic—within cultures as the defining characteristics of four different evolutionary stages. The types of integration are seen as the major factor forcing cultures to higher levels of evolutionary development. Bands, the lowest level, occur when no form of social, political, or economic integration exists between local groups. Tribes, the next level, are defined by the existence of pantribal sodalities which are kinship groups including in their memberships individuals from different local groups. Reciprocity between local groups may occur at this level. Chiefdoms exist, by definition, when there is redistribution through a nonlocal allocative center. A chief presides over the administrative center. Political force need not be present for redistribution to occur. States arise when there develops a government with the legitimate use of force. Market exchange is often characteristic of states. Although Service uses social and political criteria, as well as an economic criterion, for establishing his different forms of integration, he has made a strong argument for the importance of studying the economic integration of a culture, particularly integration based upon redistribution through a nonlocal allocative agency.

9. **Which principle of exchange is integrative for the entire culture?**
    1. none; that is, no patterned exchange between local groups
    2. balanced reciprocity between local groups

3. generalized reciprocity between local groups
4. redistribution through a nonlocal allocative center
5. market exchange

The same definitions as given in the previous section hold for these principles of exchange. They differ, however, in the unit to which they are being applied. In the first instance the terms were used to classify the economic system of the local group, and in this section they are used to classify the form of economic integration within the culture.

Balanced reciprocity occurs between Yąnomamö local groups (Chagnon 1968:100):

> Three distinct features of Yąnomamö trading practices are important in the context of alliance formation. First, each item must be repaid with a different kind of item. . . . Secondly, the payment is delayed. . . . The consequence of these two trading features is that one trade always calls forth another and gives the members of different villages both the excuse and the opportunity to visit each other. . . . The third significant trade feature is the peculiar specialization in the production of trade items. Each village has one or more special products that it provides to its allies. These include such items as dogs, hallucinogenic drugs (both cultivated and collected), arrow points, arrow shafts, bows, cotton yarn, cotton and vine hammocks, baskets of several varieties, clay pots, and, in the case of the several contacted villages, steel tools and aluminum pots.

Intervillage feasting, in addition to trading, is also an example of balanced reciprocity (Chagnon 1968:97):

> The chief purpose of entertaining allies is to reaffirm and cultivate intervillage solidarity in the intimate, sociable context of food presentations, thereby putting the ally under obligation to reciprocate the feast in his own village at a later date, bringing about another feast and even more solidarity.

In addition to market exchange, which is integrative for the entire culture of the Qemant (see Question 8), redistribution through a nonlocal allocative center also occurs (Gamst 1969:83):

> The third mode of distribution [the first two described were formal and informal marketing] ties in with Qemant religious practices and kinship, and consists of collection and redistribution, in connection with ceremonies, of beverages and raw and processed foods. Peasants contribute animals and food used by the wambar and the priests for

sacrifices and feasts. Contributions are made according to a person's means, the wealthy donating more than the poor. However, at ceremonies every participant consumes to his capacity or until the supply is exhausted. At certain times in the year, everyone in a community is thus guaranteed a feast that includes meat, which is not ordinarily part of a poor person's diet.

Gamst continues by describing a phenomenon which he considers to be redistribution, but what is more properly classified as generalized reciprocity within the local group, since a local allocative agency is absent and since the recipients are apparently not due what they receive and the givers are apparently not obliged to give (1969:83–84):

Collection and redistribution of food for use in rituals is sometimes based on kinship and membership in associations. For rites of passage, food is collected from people who are related to the persons undergoing the rites, and distributed among the members of the community.

Taxation by the Ethiopian government is also another form of redistribution, which tends however to integrate the Qemant into a modern nation rather than to integrate Qemant culture (Gamst 1969:20,71).

CHAPTER **3**

Family
and Kinship

One of the most difficult problems facing an ethnographer is to be able to distinguish between ideal and real behavior. Since much of the data collected in the field comes from the verbal accounts of individuals, it is necessary that the ethnographer ascertain whether the information is a statement of what ought to be or a recounting of what does occur. Informants will often describe to an interviewer the ideal behavior of the members of their culture in a manner which allows the interviewer to construe the response as a statement of the actual behavior. This is not usually a deliberate attempt to lie and deceive, but rather it arises from the embarrassment that the informant would feel if he told of practices which he was not proud of. The skilled ethnographer avoids confusing the ideal and the real by checking his data with other informants, by collecting actual cases in detail, by observing as much actual behavior as possible, and by collecting census and genealogical data. If this is done, the monograph prepared by the ethnographer will distinguish between those statements describing what ought to be and those describing what is.

In no realm of anthropology is it more important to distinguish between ideal and real behavior than in the study of the family and kinship. An informant may tell the ethnographer where a person should live, what kind of household he should live in, how many wives he should have, whether he should marry a first cousin, what descent groups he should belong to, and how he should address certain relatives. Yet in every instance, only a small minority of the members of the culture may be actually doing what they and others think they ought to be doing. In the sections in this chapter the student should record the actual behavior or frequency of occurrence of the practices. If there is an explicit rule, norm, or ideal which does or does not correspond with the actual practice, it should also be recorded.

Residence

Marital residence has been an important topic of anthropological research since the latter part of the nineteenth century. Edward B. Tylor (1888), in what is probably the most outstanding article ever to be written by an anthropologist, distinguished three types of marital residence and showed their relationship to several different kinship customs. The three types of residence were also related to stages of cultural evolution. According to Tylor (1888:247), at the lowest stage of cultural development the husband took up "his abode with the wife's family permanently," at a higher stage he did so "temporarily and eventually to remove with her to his own family or home (the reverse of this does not occur)," and at the highest stage "the husband takes his wife to his home." Today these modes of residence are known respectively as matrilocal, matri-patrilocal, and patrilocal residence. For Tylor matri-patrilocal residence was referred to as transitional or removal; the other two types were left unnamed. The recent "classic" statement on residence comes from George P. Murdock in his book *Social Structure* (1949). He defines *matrilocal* residence as occurring if the groom leaves "his parental home and live[s] with his bride, either in the house of her parents or in a dwelling nearby" (1949:16). *Patrilocal* residence occurs if "the bride regularly removes to or near the parental home of the groom" (1949:16). Murdock proposes the term *matri-patrilocal* residence for the combination in which matrilocal residence occurs "for an initial period, usually for a year or until the birth of the first child, to be followed by permanent patrilocal residence" (1949:17). He considers this form of residence "only a special variant of patrilocal residence" (1949:17).

In addition to defining the above three modes of residence, Murdock describes two other forms of marital residence. In *avunculocal* residence the couple "reside with or near a maternal uncle of the groom rather than with the parents of either spouse or in a separate home of their own" (1949:17). The most difficult form of residence to understand is *bilocal* or *ambilocal* residence, since the practice refers not to a single couple but to all the married couples in the culture or the local group. "Some societies permit a married couple to live with or near the parents of either spouse, in which case such factors as the relative wealth or status of the two families or the personal preferences of the parties to the union are likely to determine whether they will choose to reside matrilocally or patrilocally" (1949:16). Thus individual couples practice either patrilocal or matrilocal residence—they themselves do not practice ambilocal residence. This form of residence pertains to the frequency of both patrilocal and matrilocal residence in a local group or in the culture as a whole. Recently Murdock

(1967:156) has helped to clarify the situation by stating that ambilocal residence is "residence established optionally with or near the parents of either the husband or the wife . . . where neither alternative exceeds the other in actual frequency by a ratio of greater than two to one." The phrase "with or near" in the above definitions is interpreted to mean within the household of the parents.

The types of residence described above involve a move by one of the marital partners from his or her parental home to the parental home of the other partner (or to the home of the groom's maternal uncle). Thus new households are not formed. What occurs is a change in the composition of the membership of the parental households. (The nature of the changes which occur will be discussed in the section titled "Household Type.") On the other hand, there are four types of residence which do lead to the formation of new households. Best known of these types is neolocal residence. Murdock has defined *neolocal* residence as "normal residence apart from the relatives of both spouses or at a place not determined by the kin ties of either" (1967:156). Two other types of residence, which produce new households, are virilocal and uxorilocal residence. *Virilocal* residence means that the "married couple customarily becomes part of the male's natal residence group"; *uxorilocal* residence means that the "couple customarily becomes part of the female's natal group" (Service 1962:30). The use of the term natal is ambiguous since it can refer either to the household or the local group into which one is born. All three of the above definitions can be rendered more precise by considering the various logical alternatives open to a married man and woman who are establishing their own household. They may establish their household in a local group other than the local group or groups where their parental homes are located (neolocal residence). They may establish their household in a local group in which the man's parental home is located, but not the woman's parental home (virilocal residence). They may establish their household in a local group in which the woman's parental home is located, but not the man's parental home (uxorilocal residence). A fourth logical alternative exists— they may establish their household in the same local group in which the parental homes of both the man and the woman are located. For this type of residence I propose the term *commonlocal*. Although marriage within the local group has been referred to as "local endogamy," the expression does not distinguish between residence involving the establishment of a new household and residence in which one partner moves into the parental home of the other partner.

An ethnographer in the field is faced with the task of ascertaining what form of residence is being practiced by each married couple in the local group or groups he is studying. (Criteria for identifying marital unions will be discussed in the next section.) When this is completed he must tabulate the frequency with which each type of residence occurs. For classifying a culture as to the type of residence which prevails, the frequencies are used. Table 1 shows the classification of cultures, based upon the frequency ranges (in percentages) of practices followed by individual couples. (The frequency ranges are derived from Murdock's recent definition of ambilocal residence.) In order to determine the residence practice

Table 1.   Classification of Cultures by Individual Couples

Type of Residence	Type of Residence Practiced by Couples	Percentage Practicing
Ambilocal	Patrilocal and	33 – 66
	Matrilocal	33 – 66
Patrilocal	Patrilocal and	67–100
	All other types of residence combined	0 – 33
Matrilocal	Matrilocal and	67–100
	All other types of residence combined	0 – 33
Avunculocal	Avunculocal and	67–100
	All other types of residence combined	0 – 33
Neolocal	Neolocal and	67–100
	All other types of residence combined	0 – 33
Virilocal	Virilocal and	67–100
	All other types of residence combined	0 – 33
Uxorilocal	Uxorilocal and	67–100
	All other types of residence combined	0 – 33
Commonlocal	Commonlocal and	67–100
	All other types of residence combined	0 – 33

of a culture, it is necessary to locate in the ethnography the most detailed enumeration of the types of residence practiced by individual couples. Sometimes this information is found in a table, sometimes in a statement to the effect that a certain percentage or frequency of the people reside according to one of the types of residence. In older ethnographies, when it was not the practice for ethnographers to take a detailed census, one may find only a statement that residence is either patrilocal, matrilocal, or neo-local (ambilocal, avunculocal, virilocal, uxorilocal, and commonlocal are newer terms). The residence data, converted to percentages if necessary, are compared with the right-hand side of the chart. For example, if 60 percent of the couples reside patrilocally and 40 percent matrilocally, the culture is classified as ambilocal. However, if 80 percent of the couples reside patrilocally and only 20 percent reside matrilocally, then the culture is classified as patrilocal. If the residence data consists of frequencies of types of residence which do not fit the right-hand side of the chart, these frequencies should be recorded and no attempt should be made to classify the culture according to one of the eight residence practices.

Matri-patrilocal residence, which is not shown on the chart, presents a problem in classification, since a local group practicing this form of residence would show at a particular point in time some couples residing matrilocally and the remainder residing patrilocally. It would be a mistake to classify the culture as ambilocal, since the couples residing matrilocally will soon be residing patrilocally. Probably the best procedure to follow is to classify instances of matri-patrilocal residence as patrilocal residence. This can be done if the ethnographer states in his census of the types of residence being practiced that certain couples residing matrilocally will soon be residing patrilocally. Thus matri-patrilocal residence is not shown on the chart.

10. **What type of marital residence is practiced?**
    1. ambilocal
    2. patrilocal
    3. matrilocal
    4. avunculocal
    5. neolocal
    6. virilocal
    7. uxorilocal
    8. commonlocal

The above discussion of residence has focused upon only the real or actual behavior of individual couples, although much of the literature in anthropology which deals with marital residence, including Murdock's treatment, concerns itself primarily with the ideal—that is, with the explicit cultural rules which state what people ought to do (Bohannan 1963:86–99). Thus many discussions of residence are discussions of marital residence rules. It is important to know what the rules are (if indeed there are such rules) and whether the actual residence of individual couples conforms or does not conform to the rules. In understanding any culture it is crucial to know why conformity does or does not occur. Thus not only should one record the type of residence practiced, but he should also note what the residence rules are if they are explicitly stated in the ethnography. Such rules will read the same as the definitions of the eight types of residence, with the addition of a phrase such as "the couple should," "custom requires," or "the husband is expected to."

A Yąnomamö male upon marriage usually establishes his own household within the village in which he grew up (see Question 6). His wife is likely to be a cross-cousin (see Question 15) from the same village. If she is not a member of his village or he marries a nonrelative in another village, he will probably have to perform bride service, perhaps for as long as three years. During this period the husband lives in his wife's village and hunts for his wife and her parents (Chagnon 1968:79,93). Hence, for some men residence is initially matrilocal. Some wives are obtained by abduction (Chagnon 1968:73,98). Thus the vast majority (exact figures are not given) of Yąnomamö men reside in their own village. Their wives are from the same or a different village. Many anthropologists would classify the Yąnomamö as patrilocal; however, Chagnon refrains from using residence concepts such as patrilocal. Strict adherence to the above definitions requires that the Yąnomamö be classified as having both commonlocal and virilocal residence, since a man establishes his own household upon marriage and remains in the local group in which his parental home is located. Since one cannot be certain that over 67 percent of the men are residing commonlocally, the Yąnomamö cannot be classified as either commonlocal or virilocal. Hence both types of residence should be recorded.

Marital residence for the Qemant is initially patrilocal, then becomes virilocal or commonlocal (Gamst 1969:109–110):

> If a girl is past puberty at the time of her marriage, she usually resides with the groom at his father's house. . . .
> After several years of marriage, a couple builds its own house and sets up a household next to that of the groom's parents.

However, if the bride has not reached puberty, she continues to live with her parents while the groom continues to live with his parents (Gamst 1969:109–110).

Gamst describes Qemant marital residence with the following technical terms (1969:69):

> Residence after marriage but before the newlywed couple builds a house is duolocai at first, the groom living with his parents and the bride with her parents. Residence then gradually becomes patrilocal or, at

times, matrilocal, the married couple living with the groom's parents or with the bride's parents. . . . Residence after construction of a house is usually patrilocal; a son builds a house near that of his father after approximately three to five years of marriage.

Elsewhere Gamst states that (1969:26):

Patrilocality (residence of a married couple with or near the groom's parents) is the nominal rule, although it is followed only about seventy percent of the time. In practice, a man may build his house anywhere, given sufficient incentive (options on the land of his wife's family or a relative's family, or strife within his own family).

Gamst, it should be noted, is using the term patrilocal in its earlier more general sense. Thus his use of the term includes patrilocal, virilocal, and commonlocal. Since information concerning which communities men take their wives from is lacking, it is not possible to determine whether virilocal or commonlocal residence is the prevailing mode of marital residence. Probably—and this is only a guess—most men obtain wives from their own local group; however, some men may be forced to seek wives from other local groups because of restrictions imposed by kinship and religion. Since none of the types of marital residence described above appear to exceed 67 percent, all four types should be recorded—patrilocal, matrilocal, virilocal, and commonlocal. "Duolocal" residence, mentioned by Gamst, should not be regarded as a type of marital residence, since the bride and groom are not living together. In fact, common residence is one criterion for distinguishing marital unions (see "Marriage").

Marriage

Marriage is a sexual relationship between a man and woman who share a common residence. The relationship is to be distinguished both from casual mating and from relatively permanent sexual relationships which do not involve living together. On the other hand, living together does not constitute marriage unless the man and the woman are sexual partners. For marriage to exist two criteria must be satisfied: presence of a sexual relationship and common residence. The marital relationship is sometimes referred to as the conjugal tie (Fox 1967:39–40) or the conjugal dyad (Adams 1960:39). Marriage is also referred to as an affinal relationship. When a man and woman enter into marriage, a social unit or entity—a marital group—is formed. The above definition of marriage can be referred to as a common sense definition; it corresponds to what most of us think of as marriage. Some anthropologists, however, do not regard this definition

of marriage as satisfactory since there are some cultures—very few—
which do not have marriage or marital groups in terms of the above definitions. These anthropologists prefer a definition which is applicable to all
cultures (Malinowski 1930:140; Gough 1959:32; Goodenough 1970:12–
13). Although the common sense definition may not be universally
applicable, such a definition, based upon two criteria, permits the delinea-
tion of different types of marriage, or rather marital groups.

The types of marriage found among the different peoples of the
world are known by nearly everyone—monogamy, polygyny, and polyandry. *Monogamy* is the marriage of one man to one woman; *polygyny* is
the marriage of one man to two or more women at one time; *polyandry* is
the marriage of one woman to two or more men at one time. (The term
polygamy refers to either polygyny or polyandry.) What is not usually
realized, however, is that these types of marriage do not pertain to individual marital unions but to the composition of marital groups. That is,
the type of marriage does not affect the nature of the marital relationship,
as defined above. Rather, the terms refer to the social groups which are
formed when individual men and women enter into one or more marital
unions. This point can probably be more easily grasped if the composition
of each of the three types of marital groups is diagramed. The following
symbols, employed by virtually all anthropologists, are utilized in the
diagrams: △ (triangle) = male; ◯ (circle) = female; = (equal sign) =
marital union.

Type of Marriage	Diagram Showing Composition of Marital Group	Definition
Monogamy	△ = ◯	male married to female
Polygyny	◯ = △ = ◯	male married to two females
Polyandry	△ = ◯ = △	female married to two males

Logically a fourth type of marital group can occur. This would consist of
two or more men being married to two or more women at one time.
Such a group can be diagramed as follows:

$$\begin{matrix} △ & = & ◯ \\ \| & & \| \\ ◯ & = & △ \end{matrix}$$

Following the practice of nineteenth-century anthropologists, this type of
marital group can be called *group marriage*. However, ethnographic research has demonstrated that group marriage has never occurred as the

prevailing type of marital group in any culture. A fifth type of marital group can be derived from the diagram for group marriage if a marital union does not exist between one of the men and one of the women:

$$\triangle \overset{=}{\underset{\shortparallel}{}} \bigcirc$$
$$\bigcirc = \triangle$$

Such a group can be labeled polyandry-polygyny. I know of only one culture in which such marital groups were frequently found—the Marquesan Islanders of the South Pacific (Otterbein 1963).

Some cultures are 100 percent monogamous; that is, only monogamous marital groups are found present in the culture. Such a situation usually occurs because of a rule which prohibits an individual from having more than one spouse at one time. However, a majority of the world's cultures permit men to be married to more than one woman at one time. Thus many cultures contain polygynous marital groups. Since it is rare to find a culture in which every married man has more than one wife (a man usually marries one wife, then later another), most cultures containing polygynous marital groups also contain monogamous marital groups. On the other hand, it is rare to find a culture which permits a man to have more than one wife, and yet which contains only monogamous marital groups. Polyandrous marital groups are rarely found. Few cultures permit a woman to be married to two or more men at one time. When it is permitted, the two men are often brothers. Such a practice is known as *fraternal polyandry*. When polyandrous marital groups are discovered, the culture is also likely to contain both monogamous and polygynous marital groups. One study of 554 cultures found that 24 percent of the world's cultures were monogamous, 75 percent were polygynous, and 1 percent were polyandrous (Murdock 1957:686).

Just as an ethnographer needs to ascertain the type of residence being practiced by each married couple in the local group, he also needs to describe the composition of the marital groups to which the married couples belong. Each married individual will belong to one, and only one, marital group at one time. Monogamous groups, of course, will consist of only two individuals, while polygynous and polyandrous groups will vary in size from three to perhaps hundreds of individuals (if one man has hundreds of wives). Each marital group can be classified according to one of the three types of marriage. Then the frequency of each type of marital group can be tabulated. Although most ethnographers do not present the data in their monographs in terms of the number of marital groups conforming to each type of marriage, they often do provide information on the number of wives each man has. Since each married man belongs to a different marital group, except where polyandry occurs, the number of men with only one wife provides us with the number of monogamous marital unions and the number of men with more than one wife provides us with the number of polygynous marital unions. The figures can be used to compute percentages. If all (100 percent) of the marital groups in the culture are monogamous, the culture is classified as practicing *monogamy*. If the percentage of polygynous marital groups in a culture ranges between 1 and 19 percent, the culture is classified as practicing *limited polygyny*; if the percentage of polygynous marital groups ranges from 20 to 100 percent, the culture is classified as practicing *general polygyny* (Murdock 1957:670–671). Twenty percent is an arbitrary dividing line which roughly separates cultures practicing polygyny into two equal groups. If there are polyandrous marital groups in the culture, the culture is classified as practicing *polyandry*.

11. What type of marriage is practiced?
   1. monogamy
   2. limited polygyny
   3. general polygyny
   4. polyandry

The type of marriage practiced is determined by the percentage of the different types of marital groups in the culture. The actual percentages should be recorded. If the culture does not have marriage and marital groups are absent—and it is rare to find such cultures—the absence of marriage should be noted.

———————

General polygyny is practiced by the Yąnomamö. Although exact figures are not given, it appears that well over 20 percent of the marital groups are polygynous (Chagnon 1968:73,75). A case is described in which the village headman shares his house with his youngest brother, and he also "shares" his younger wife with his brother (Chagnon 1968: 14,89). This appears to be a case of fraternal polyandry. However, the arrangement is probably temporary, and hence the marital group does not warrant being classified as polyandrous.

The Qemant practice monogamy (Gamst 1969:67):

Marriage among the Qemant is monogamous. Concubinage exists, but there is now no polygyny, although Qemant legends, Ethiopic manuscripts, and early European accounts mention this practice.

Household Type

A household is a group of people living together who form a domestic unit. Usually the group occupies a physical structure with walls and a roof which can be described as a house or homestead. In some instances, however, the household may occupy a unit in a larger structure, or the household may occupy several houses, usually adjacent. The people occupying the house must cooperate in domestic and subsistence tasks for a household to exist. That is, the members of a household cook, eat, sleep, and work together—they can be said to share a common hearth. The basis of this cooperation is usually a division of labor characterized by age and sex. Most households are composed of married men and women and their offspring. Thus, in addition to domestic economic cooperation, the household usually performs three other functions: sexual gratification, reproduction and child care, and socialization of children (Murdock 1949:7–11). Although it is possible to have households or residential groups which consist of nonrelated individuals, the types of households described below are composed of individuals related by kinship and marriage. Diagrams will be used to show the social composition of each household type. The three symbols introduced in the previous section will be used, plus two additional symbols:

| (a vertical line) = the relationship of descent
⌐ (an inverted bracket) = the sibling relationship

The diagrams used to illustrate household composition are enclosed in rectangles which symbolize the physical structure in which households live.

The type of household characteristic of a culture depends primarily upon the type of marital groups present and the mode of residence practiced. Independent nuclear family households are formed when monogamous marital groups and neolocal, virilocal, uxorilocal, or commonlocal residence occur together. By definition monogamy means that there will be only one husband and one wife living in the household, and neolocal, virilocal, uxorilocal, or commonlocal residence means that the couple and any children resulting from the union will reside in a house independent of the parental home of either spouse. A household with the following composition results:

The diagram shows a husband, a wife, and two children, a brother and a sister. The square enclosing the diagram symbolizes the house in which the parents and children reside. Thus an *independent nuclear family household* is a domestic group consisting of a married couple and their children who occupy a dwelling which is not part of any other household. Independent polygamous family households occur when either polygynous or polyandrous marital groups and neolocal, virilocal, uxorilocal, or commonlocal residence prevail within a culture. If the marital group is polygynous, there will be one husband, two or more wives, and their children living in the household. A household with the following structure results:

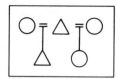

If the marital group is polyandrous, there will be one wife, her children, and two or more husbands living in the household. Such a household can be diagramed as follows:

(Although it is usually not possible to determine the biological father of each child when polyandry occurs, one husband is shown as the father of the children in the diagram.) Thus an *independent polygamous family household* is a domestic group consisting of either a polygynous or a polyandrous marital group and its children who occupy a dwelling which is not part of any other household. Both independent nuclear family households and independent polygamous family households contain two generations of related individuals.

Extended family households come into existence when marital residence is other than neolocal, virilocal, uxorilocal, or commonlocal. Either patrilocal, matrilocal, or avunculocal residence can produce extended family households. These three types of residence include in their definitions the statement that the couple live "with or near" either the groom's parents, the bride's parents, or the maternal uncle of the groom. The phrase with or near means that the couple takes up residence within the household—not necessarily the same dwelling, since a household may occupy several houses—of the designated relative. The practice of either patrilocal, matrilocal, or avunculocal residence draws together into one household three or more generations of related individuals. Extended family households can be classified by the type of residence practiced: patrilocal extended family households, matrilocal extended family households, and avunculocal extended family households. An extended family household of the patrilocal variety can be diagramed as follows:

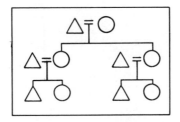

If the type of residence practiced is matrilocal, the household will have the following structure:

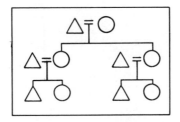

A culture characterized by ambilocal residence will have extended family households of both the patrilocal and matrilocal variety. There may also occur in such cultures extended family households in which both sons and daughters have brought their spouses to reside in their paternal household. These ambilocal extended family households arise when a son resides patrilocally and a daughter resides matrilocally. (Diagrams of ambilocal and avunculocal extended family households are not presented.) Although it would be possible to distinguish between extended nuclear family households and extended polygamous family households on the basis of the type of marital groups included in the households (as was done for independent households above), anthropologists have not made this distinction. Thus an *extended family household* is a domestic group consisting of three (or possibly more) generations of related individuals, including one or more marital groups in each of two adjacent generations. It does not matter whether the marital groups composing the household are monogamous, polygynous, or polyandrous.

A subtype of the extended family household has been distinguished by anthropologists. The stem family household comes into existence when only one child of a marital group remains in the household and brings his or her spouse to reside there. Either patrilocal or matrilocal residence can produce stem family households. If patrilocal residence is practiced, such households have the following composition:

If matrilocal residence is practiced, the household can be diagramed as follows:

Thus the *stem family household* is a small extended family household consisting of three generations of related individuals, including one marital group in each of two adjacent generations.

Two other types of households are occasionally described by anthropologists. One is the *fraternal joint family household* composed of two or more brothers, their wives, and their children (Murdock 1949:33); the other is the *mother-child* or *female headed household* composed of a woman, who is either unmarried, widowed, separated, or divorced, and her children, and sometimes her grandchildren (Otterbein 1965b). The former type is comparatively rare, and the latter type is probably never found as the dominant household type in any culture.

Many ethnographers who collect information on residence and marital groups also collect information on household composition. In some cases the composition of every household in the local group is presented in the ethnography. Other times the ethnographer derives household types for the culture and presents the frequency of each type in a table. Sometimes he simply describes the major household type and any variations from the type. Although households vary greatly in size and in composition, for most cultures one type of household is dominant. That is, most of the households in the culture will conform to one of the major types of households described above.

12. What types of households are present?
1. independent nuclear family
2. independent polygamous family
3. extended family
4. stem family

The most frequently occurring type of household should be noted. If there is a less common type occurring with some regularity, it should also be recorded. The type of household that people prefer to live in may not be the most frequently occurring type. Thus the evaluations which members of the culture hold concerning household composition should be noted, if this information is available in the ethnography. The variations on each major household type do not need to be listed, since data on residence and marital groups, recorded for the two previous sections, provide this information.

Since commonlocal and virilocal residence are practiced by the Yąnomamö and many of the marital groups are polygynous, independent polygamous family households occur with great frequency. On the other hand, men with only one wife reside in independent nuclear family households. Thus both types of households are present. Exact figures on household composition are not given. However, since it is unlikely that polygynous marital groups exceed 50 percent of the marital groups, probably independent nuclear family households are the most frequently occurring type.

The virilocal and commonlocal residence of the Qemant, in conjunction with monogamous marital groups, produces independent nuclear family households. Extended family households are also present because both patrilocal and matrilocal residence are practiced. Although exact figures on household composition are not given, independent nuclear family households probably occur with greater frequency. Since Qemant reside patrilocally or matrilocally for only the first few years of their married life, a married man and woman spend the greater part of their lives apart from their parents, with only their children present in the household. Not until one of their children brings a spouse into the household does their nuclear family household become converted into an extended family household.

Descent Groups

Many cultures have descent groups; membership in these groups is determined by a rule of descent. A descent group is "any publicly recognized social entity such that being a lineal descendant of a particular real or fictive ancestor is a criterion of membership" (Goodenough 1970:51). Descent, on the other hand, refers "solely to a cultural principle whereby an individual is socially allocated to a specific group of consanguineal kinsmen" (Murdock 1949:43). Such kinsmen are descended from a common ancestor. Allocation to a descent group, known technically as filiation, is through either one's father or one's mother. Descent groups and rules of descent go hand in hand; that is, it is impossible to have one without the other. Four basic types of descent groups and rules of descent can be distinguished:

Descent Group	Rule of Descent
Patrilineage	Patrilineal descent
Matrilineage	Matrilineal descent
Ambilineage	Ambilineal descent
Unrestricted descent group	Multilineal descent

All four types of descent groups are similar in their fundamental structure: they are multigenerational; they are headed or founded by an ancestor (sometimes they are referred to as ancestor-oriented groups); and they include in their membership only descendants of the ancestor. These four types of groups differ in their structure or composition because of different rules of descent. With the exception of multilineal descent, rules of descent are a means of limiting membership in descent groups. They prescribe who can and who cannot belong. The members of a patrilineage, a matrilineage, an ambilineage, or an unrestricted descent group are usually referred to by a certain name, and in most cultures they regularly assist each other in economic, political, and religious matters (Befu and Plotnicov 1962).

Membership in a patrilineage is based upon a rule of *patrilineal descent*. This cultural principle automatically filiates a child at birth through his father to a descent group that consists of all kinsmen who are related to him through his male ancestor. An individual will belong to only one patrlineage, and the members of a lineage may reside in different local groups. A patrilineage has the following structure:

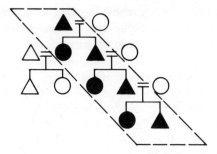

Members of the patrilineage are shown in black, and they are enclosed within a dotted parallelogram in order to indicate that patrilineages are usually nonlocalized groups. In the diagram individuals are shown marrying spouses who are not members of their patrilineage. Thus a *patrilineage* is a descent group whose membership is based upon a rule of patrilineal descent. Because patrilineages are similar in structure to patrilocal extended family households, many anthropologists believe that patrilineages may have developed out of patrilocal extended family households which have grown larger and larger through the birth of individuals who belong to new generations (Titiev 1943).

Membership in a matrilineage is based upon a rule of *matrilineal descent*. This cultural principle automatically filiates a child at birth through his mother to a descent group that consists of all kinsmen who are related to him through his female ancestors. A matrilineage has the following structure:

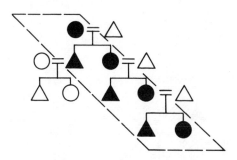

Thus a *matrilineage* is a descent group whose membership is based upon a rule of matrilineal descent. Many anthropologists believe that matrilineages have grown out of matrilocal extended family households, just as patrilineages have grown out of patrilocal extended family households.

Membership in an ambilineage, sometimes referred to as a ramage, is based upon a rule of *ambilineal descent*. This cultural principle filiates an individual through either his father or mother to a descent group that consists of only some of his kinsmen. Filiation does not necessarily occur at birth, but is more likely to occur in adulthood. Residence, which plays no role in determining membership in patrilineages and matrilineages, is usually the deciding factor in determining the parent through whom filiation will be traced. This is because ambilineages are almost always land-owning groups, and an individual must live with other members of the ambilineage and till the soil in order to exercise his right to belong to the ambilineage. In some cultures his membership may be determined by the residence of his parents. If they reside with his paternal grandparents, he will filiate through his father and belong to his father's ambilineage; if they reside with his maternal grandparents, he will filiate through his mother and belong to his mother's ambilineage. This occurs only if he resides with his parents as a child and as an adult. If after marriage he resides with his spouse's parents, he does not exercise his right to belong to an ambilineage. His children will filiate through their mother. Such ambilineages are said to be of the exclusive or irreversible type. There are also ambilineages of a nonexclusive or reversible type. In the nonexclusive type an individual can always reverse his choice; that is, after having lived with one ambilineage for several years he can change his membership to the other ambilineage by making a change of residence. Thus, an individual always retains his rights to belong to two different ambilineages regardless of his residence (Otterbein 1964:32).

Since ambilineages—in contrast to either patrilineages or matri-lineages—have variable structure, two examples are given, one headed by a male, the other by a female.

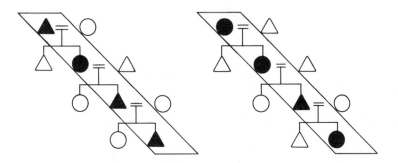

Members of the ambilineages are shown in black, and each ambilineage is enclosed within a solid parallelogram to emphasize that ambilineages are usually localized groups. Thus an *ambilineage* or *ramage* is a descent group whose membership is based upon a rule of ambilineal descent. Since ambilineal descent groups derive their structure from the residential choices

of individuals, ambilocal residence is usually found associated with ambilineages and ambilineal descent. (It will be remembered that a culture
which has couples residing both patrilocally and matrilocally is classified
as practicing ambilocal residence.) Presumably ambilineages grow out of
ambilocal extended family households.

The unrestricted descent group is based upon a rule of *multilineal
descent*. From the point of view of the founder of an unrestricted descent
group, multilineal descent refers to all of his descendants, not his ancestors
or collateral relatives. This cultural principle automatically filiates a child
at birth through his father and his mother (and through his four grandparents, and through his eight great grandparents, and so on) to every
descent group founded by one of his ancestors. An unrestricted descent
group has the following structure:

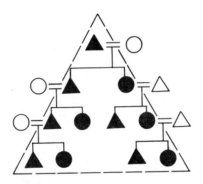

Members of the unrestricted descent group are shown in black, and they
are enclosed within a dotted triangle in order to indicate that such descent
groups are nonlocalized. An individual can belong to many of these nonlocalized descent groups, and the type of residence which he practices has
no effect on his memberships. Thus an *unrestricted descent group* is a
descent group whose membership is based upon a rule of multilineal descent
(Otterbein 1964).

In addition to these four basic types of descent groups, three other
types of descent groups—based upon lineages—have been distinguished.
The term *lineage* refers to both patrilineages and matrilineages. In many
cultures lineages are found joined together into larger descent groups. A
clan exists when the members of two or more lineages consider their
lineages to be units or segments of a larger descent group. Clans are
nonlocalized, they are named, and they are based upon the same rule of
descent as the lineages which compose them. If clans are united into an
even larger descent group which is nonlocalized, which is named, and which
is based upon the same rule of descent as the clans composing it, a *phratry*

occurs. If there are more than three levels of kinship units in a descent group, ethnographers usually develop their own notational system for describing each level. If the culture has only two clans or two phratries, so that every individual is a member of one or the other, the culture is said to have moieties. Each clan or phratry is referred to as a *moiety*. Since lineages compose clans and clans compose phratries, it is not possible to have phratries without clans and lineages, nor is it possible to have clans without lineages.

13. What types of descent groups are present?
1. descent groups absent
2. patrilineages
3. matrilineages
4. ambilineages
5. unrestricted descent groups
6. clans
7. phratries
8. moieties

Not all cultures have descent groups, and those that do usually have only one of the above four basic types. There are some cultures, however, which have both patrilineages and matrilineages. These cultures are said by anthropologists to practice *double descent*. Rarely will lineages be found in cultures with ambilineages. Unrestricted descent groups may be found in cultures with ambilineages, but probably never in cultures with lineages. Clans, phratries, and moieties may be based upon either patrilineal or matrilineal descent. It has not been necessary to list patriclans, matriclans, patriphratries, matriphratries, patrimoieties, and matrimoieties above, since information on the type of descent rule followed by one of these groups is contained in the prefix of the type of lineages composing the larger descent group. The above question simply asks what types of descent groups are present—it does not ask how many descent groups of each type are present (except indirectly by asking about moieties), nor does it ask how many members each descent group has. If this latter information is given in the ethnography, it is worth noting.

––––––––––

Patrilineages are the only type of descent group which the Yąnomamö have. Two important features of their lineage system are as follows (Chagnon 1968:61):

> First, people reckon descent through males and are grouped into exogamous, patrilineal lineages. These are called *mashi* by the Yąnomamö, although none of them bear distinctive names. Second, members of these lineages tend to intermarry with members of a second

lineage over a number of generations, being bound to them by obligations to reciprocate women in marriage. This results in a dual organization of kinsmen within the village, whose residents fall into one or the
other of the two lineages.

The term *dual organization* is often used to describe moieties. If approximately half the Yąnomamö lineages were joined together into a larger
descent group and the remaining lineages were joined together into another
descent group, then moieties would be present. But such second-order
descent groups are not present, and therefore, the Yąnomamö should not be
classified as having moieties. Since there are no second-order descent groups,
clans are absent.

The "local descent group" described by Chagnon is a smaller kinship
group than the patrilineage. It cannot be classified as a lineage, an ambilineage, or an unrestricted descent group, since coresidence, in addition to
patrilineal descent, is a criterion for membership (Chagnon 1968:68–69):

> Local descent groups have three characteristics. First, membership in
> them depends on patrilineal descent. . . . Second, the members of the
> group live in the same village. If, for example, a young man leaves his
> village to seek a wife elsewhere, he is no longer a member of the
> local descent group that includes his brothers and father. He can rejoin
> them later and again become an active member, but while he lives in
> a different village he does not participate in the political affairs of that
> group. Third, the group is *corporate* with respect to the functions of
> arranging the marriages of the female members.

The Qemant have patrilineages, clans, and moieties (Gamst 1969:3):

> The males of each homestead are closely related through paternal lines
> to one another and to males in some of the nearby homesteads in their
> community. The paternal lines lead back to the oldest living male among
> them or to an ancestor of these men from one or two generations earlier.
> These paternal lines can be traced back through time, along with many
> other such lines of descent from part of the remainder of the community
> and from parts of other Qemant communities, until they ultimately
> merge into the person of a culture hero who is the common ancestor
> of this vast number of men and the founder of the clan to which they
> belong. Therefore, a clan is a kinship group whose members trace
> descent unilineally, through the line of one parent—in this case, the
> male line—to an ancestor who is usually mythical.
>
> The many Qemant clans, each composed of several lineages, or seg-
> ments of the clan, are united on a greater structural level to form two
> moieties, a fundamental dual social division into which an ethnic group
> may be organized. All Qemant belong to either one or the other of the

two moieties, and they must marry, according to Qemant marriage laws, outside of their own moiety and into the other one; these moieties are therefore exogamous.

Gamst uses the concept of ambilineal in his discussion of land tenure and the inheritance of property (1969:70):

> Rights to the use of land are based upon kinship traced ambilineally, as in the following sentences which explain ambilineality. In justifying or establishing claims to use land, any of the sixteen great-great-grand-parents may be used, and rights to land are usually traced to still more distant ancestors. Claims are made through a single line of descent traced generation after generation back and forth in any way from male to female ancestors, hence ambilineally, to the ancestor who first cultivated the land.

Although he speaks of a person's "ambilineal descent group," the Qemant appear not to have ambilineages, since distinct ancestor-oriented groups based upon a rule of ambilineal descent are not discussed. What Gamst describes as an ambilineal descent group should probably be classified as a kindred (See Question 14).

Kindreds

In contrast to descent groups, which are ancestor-oriented, are kindreds or ego-oriented aggregates of individuals. A kindred is an aggregate rather than a social group because its membership is composed of individuals who define their respective membership in the aggregate in terms of their relationship to a particular individual, technically known as *Ego*. In a group, on the other hand, each individual has a relationship with every other member of the group. In a kindred the only relationships are those between Ego and every other member of the aggregate. An ego-oriented aggregate, if its membership includes only kinsmen, may consist of any of an individual's relatives, including descendants, ancestors, and collaterals such as siblings and cousins. An ancestor-oriented group (that is, a descent group) will consist of only the descendants of a particular individual, who headed or founded the group. Until, approximately a decade ago, kindreds were considered to be descent groups, which were character-ized by a rule of bilateral descent. But since their structure differs markedly from the structure of descent groups, anthropologists today consider kindreds to be a distinct kinship phenomenon which should not be classified with descent groups. Since kindreds are not descent groups, they cannot be characterized by descent; hence, the notion of bilateral descent is disappearing from usage (Buchler and Selby 1968:88–89; Mitchell 1963).

Two types of kindreds can be distinguished: (1) A kindred, as a category of kin, consists of all recognized relatives of an individual. The individual knows who should belong to his kindred and their relationship to him. The members of such a kindred constitute an aggregate which an individual can usually scan in order to find support or assistance for any activity or difficulty in which he has become involved. For an anthropologist to infer that kindreds of this type are present in a culture, the relatives composing the ego-oriented aggregate must constitute a named category. That is, the culture must have a generic name or label for this aggregate of kin. (2) A kindred, as a quasigroup, consists of those relatives of an individual who have identical rights and obligations with regard to the individual. The rights and obligations can include hospitality, responsibility for the individual's actions (such as debts and homicides), and required attendance at important ceremonial events (such as the individual's birth, initiation, wedding, and funeral). The rights and obligations are mutual since an individual belongs to the kindreds of each relative who belongs to his kindred. Kindreds, as quasigroups, are probably named, but need not be. It is possible to have more than one kind of kindred of this type (Appell 1967; Pospisil 1963:32–37,101).

Both types of kindreds are ego-oriented aggregates of relatives. It is usually stated in anthropological literature that only brothers and sisters with the same mother and father (that is, full siblings) have the same kindred. This is true for kindreds as a category of kin. It is not necessarily true for kindreds as a quasigroup, since the descendants of two siblings are related differently to each of the siblings. For example, a man is the son of his father (one sibling) but the nephew or brother's son of his father's brother (the other sibling). Thus there may be one kindred of the quasigroup type for each member of the culture. Kindreds of both types overlap in their memberships. That is, each individual will belong to many different kindreds. Kindreds of either type have traditionally been thought of as being characteristic of cultures without patrilineal or matrilineal descent groups. Although kindreds probably are more commonly found in such cultures, they nevertheless are found occasionally in cultures with descent groups.

14. What types of kindreds are present?
  1. kindreds absent
  2. kindreds, as categories of kin
  3. kindreds, as quasigroups

Determining whether kindreds are present in the culture will be a difficult task, since many ethnographers studying cultures without descent groups state that kindreds are present and that descent is bilateral. The statements of these ethnographers must be ignored. A decision as to whether kindreds are present must be made, first, on the basis of whether there is a term for all of an individual's relatives and, second, on the basis of a careful study of the rights and obligations between relatives. Careful analysis may reveal more than one kind of kindred of the quasigroup type. One must also look for kindreds in cultures with descent groups.

Kindreds of both types appear to be absent in Yąnomamö culture; no evidence for their existence can be found in the Yąnomamö ethnography.

Kindreds as quasigroups are present in Qemant culture. Although Gamst refers to a person's kinsmen as "ambilineal kin," the social relationships described in the following paragraph are entirely ego-oriented (1969:70):

> A person allows his ambilineal ties to wax and wane in strength according to his needs for labor and for support in claiming rights to use land. A Qemant may rely on local ambilineal kin to give assistance in projects requiring labor and when he is involved in a dispute. Ambilineal kin who live far away attend weddings, funerals, and other rites of passage, but may not be depended upon for labor. It is the duty of the ambilineal kin group to avenge a member's murder or to raise blood money that must be paid by a member of the group. A Qemant may be injured or murdered in revenge for an act committed by a member of his ambilineal descent group.

It can be concluded that the aggregate of kin described above is a kindred. On the other hand, no evidence is provided which could lead one to conclude that kindreds as categories of kin are present.

Cousin Marriage

In some cultures first cousins marry. Two types of cousin marriage have been distinguished by anthropologists. Parallel cousin marriage is the marriage of the children of two brothers or two sisters. An individual's father's brother's child or his mother's sister's child is his *parallel cousin.* Cross-cousin marriage is the marriage of the children of a brother and a sister. Two forms of cross-cousin marriage occur: matrilateral and patrilateral. An individual's mother's brother's child is his *matrilateral cross-cousin,* and his father's sister's child is his *patrilateral cross-cousin.*

Cross-cousin marriage may occur because there are explicit rules which state that men must or should marry a particular type of cross-cousin;

on the other hand, cross-cousin marriage may occur incidentally as a result of a rule of exogamy. Many descent groups practice *exogamy*: that is, the members of a descent group follow a rule which states that a person may not marry a member of either his lineage, clan, or phratry. The practice of exogamy produces exogamous descent groups. Exogamy may lead to cross-cousin marriage since an individual's cross-cousin is not a member of his descent group and is also a nephew or neice of one of his parents. Thus a cross-cousin is probably a likely individual for him to marry.

Matrilateral cross-cousin marriage is the marriage of a man to his mother's brother's daughter. The structure of such a marital union is shown in the following diagram:

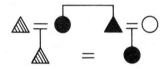

Three patrilineages are shown in different shades. In the diagram, matrilateral cross-cousin marriage is associated with lineage exogamy. Although exogamy may produce matrilateral cross-cousin marriage whether the descent groups are patrilineages or matrilineages, patrilineages are shown in the diagram, since matrilateral cross-cousin marriage is more frequently found associated with patrilineages than with matrilineages. The possible reasons for this association have created a lively debate for the last twenty years (Lévi-Strauss 1969 [orig. 1949], Homans and Schneider 1955, Needham 1960, Spiro 1968).

Patrilateral cross-cousin marriage is the marriage of a man to his father's sister's daughter. This form of marriage can be diagramed as follows:

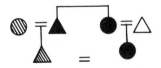

Three matrilineages are shown in different shades. Patrilateral cross-cousin marriage may occur whether matrilineages or patrilineages are present. Matrilineages are shown in this diagram since patrilateral cross-cousin marriage is more frequently found associated with matrilineages than with patrilineages. Since matrilineal descent groups occur with less frequency than patrilineal descent groups, it is to be expected that patrilateral cross-cousin marriage is a more rare form of cross-cousin marriage than the matrilateral variety. A cross-cultural study of thirty-three cultures which practice either one or the other form of cross-cousin marriage has shown that nine of the cultures had matrilineal descent groups while only seven cultures practice patrilateral cross-cousin marriage (Homans and Schneider 1955:34).

The question should be asked at this point: Why does any culture practice cross-cousin marriage? The classic and perhaps still the best answer is that cross-cousin marriage, which is associated with the practice of exogamy, is the means by which descent groups unite themselves with other descent groups (Tylor 1888:267):

> Among tribes of low culture there is but one means known of keeping up permanent alliance, and that means is intermarriage. Exogamy, enabling a growing tribe to keep itself compact by constant unions between its spreading clans, enables it to overmatch any number of small intermarrying groups, isolated and helpless. Again and again in the world's history, savage tribes must have had plainly before their minds the simple practical alternative between marrying-out and being killed out.

Parallel-cousin marriage, in comparison with cross-cousin marriage, is rare, and only the patrilateral form occurs with any frequency. Patrilateral parallel cousin marriage, usually referred to simply as *parallel cousin marriage*, is the marriage of a man to his father's brother's daughter. As is shown in the following diagram, such a marriage must—for reasons of logic—occur between members of the same descent group, provided that descent is patrilineal.

One patrilineage is shown in black. If the members of a descent group follow a rule which states that a person must marry a member of either his own lineage, clan, or phratry, a rule of *endogamy* exists. The practice of endogamy produces endogamous descent groups. Endogamous groups of course are not united by marriage with other descent groups. If it is true, as argued by Tylor, that endogamous descent groups are not likely to survive in fighting between descent groups, then groups practicing endogamy will be rare. Since parallel cousin marriage produces endogamous unions if the descent groups are patrilineal, it is to be expected that parallel cousin marriage is rarely found among the world's cultures. The only region where parallel cousin marriage occurs with any frequency is the Semitic Near East. Ethnographies which describe the cultures of the region indicate that endogamy is practiced by brothers as a technique for retaining all their inheritance within the patrilineage.

15. What types of first cousin marriage are practiced?
  1. first cousin marriage absent
  2. matrilateral cross-cousin marriage
  3. patrilateral cross-cousin marriage
  4. parallel cousin marriage

Many cultures do not practice any form of first cousin marriage. Some cultures practice only one of the types; others, a combination of both matrilateral and patrilateral cross-cousin marriage. Conceivably parallel cousin marriage can be found in association with one or both forms of cross-cousin marriage. Although the frequency with which each one of the types of first cousin marriage occurs within a given culture is important for that culture, most ethnographies do not provide the information. Frequencies, however, should be noted if they are given. In addition to frequencies, it should be noted whether an explicit marriage rule exists. Most of the theoretical literature on cross-cousin marriage has dealt with rules; however, it has been observed that most cultures practicing either matrilateral or patrilateral cross-cousin marriage "are cases in which the practice of this custom represents a personal preference of the actors rather than compliance with a rule" (Spiro 1968:113).

Both matrilateral and patrilateral cross-cousin marriage are practiced by the Yạnomamö, and there is an explicit rule which states that a man should marry a cross-cousin (Chagnon 1968:61):

Men are obliged to marry a woman of a single, specific category, *suaböya*. This category defines a variety of women, two subcategories of which can be translated into the English biological equivalents MoBrDa and FaSiDa. Yanomamö men prefer to marry women of these subcategories because they are relieved of much of the discomfort of avoiding their mother-in-law.

The ethnographer presents a table which shows that out of sixty-nine marriages, forty-four men married a cross-cousin (Chagnon 1968:73).

Neither cross-cousin nor parallel cousin marriage is practiced by the Qemant (Gamst 1969:67–68).

The incest taboo, or marriage prohibitions, among the Qemant applies to all persons in one's moiety and once included all consanguinal (blood) relatives of the other moiety less than eight degrees removed from the person. During the past forty years, Qemant have gradually reduced the prohibition to relatives only four degrees removed from one, but they still speak of the old rule as proper.

Hence, first cousin marriage is absent.

Kinship Terminology

Kinship terminological systems are classified by the terms which are employed in referring to first cousins. Although the study of kinship terminology may appear to be an obscure and esoteric subject, many of the major figures in anthropology—including Lewis H. Morgan (1871), W. H. R. Rivers (1924), A. R. Radcliffe-Brown (1952), and George P. Murdock (1949)—have considered the analysis of terminological systems crucial to an understanding of kinship and the family. Kinship terminology is viewed by most anthropologists as being a fundamental aspect of many cultures which they study. The labels for the six types of kinship systems described below are derived from the names of particular cultures or regions. Hawaiian and Eskimo stem from the Hawaiian Islanders and the Eskimo of the Arctic coast of North America. Sudanese derives from Sudan, a region south of the Sahara Desert in Africa. Iroquois, Crow, and Omaha are the names of North American Indian tribes.

The most simple terminological system is the *Hawaiian* type. All male cousins are referred to by the same term which an individual uses to refer to his brother and all female cousins are referred to by the same term which he uses to refer to his sister. If the terms for cousins differ, but are clearly derived from those for siblings, the system is still classified as Hawaiian. In the following diagram abbreviations for brother (Br) and sister (Si) are used to show that all first cousins are referred to as brother and sister:

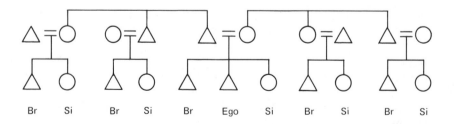

| Br | Si | Br | Si | Br | Ego | Si | Br | Si | Br | Si |

The next simplest system, familiar to most Americans, is the *Eskimo* type. Cousins are referred to by a distinctive term which is different from the term used to refer to brother and sister. In the following diagram an abbreviation for cousin (Co) is used to show that all cousins are referred to by the same term:

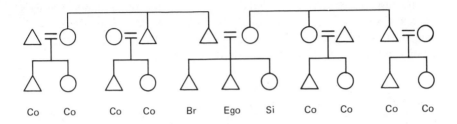

Another simple system is the *Sudanese* type. Each category of cousin is referred to by a distinct term. If the distinct terms are composed of terms used to refer to other relatives, the terminological system is said to be *descriptive*. Descriptive terminology is employed in the following diagram. Abbreviations for father (Fa), son (So), mother (Mo), and daughter (Da), in addition to brother (Br) and sister (Si), are used to show that each type of cousin is referred to by a distinct term.

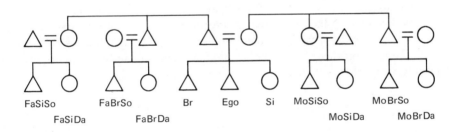

The three remaining systems are more complex than those just described. Simplest of these is the *Iroquois* type. Parallel cousins are referred to by the same terms used to refer to brother and sister, while cross-cousins are referred to by a different term.

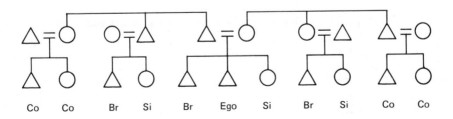

In the *Crow* type system, parallel cousins are referred to by the same terms used to refer to brother and sister, while both patrilateral and matrilateral cross-cousins have distinctive terms. Father's sister's son is referred to by the term used to refer to father, and father's sister's daughter by the term used to refer to father's sister; on the other hand, mother's brother's son is referred to as son or brother's son, and mother's brother's daughter as daughter or brother's daughter. Crow kinship systems are usually associated with matrilineal descent groups.

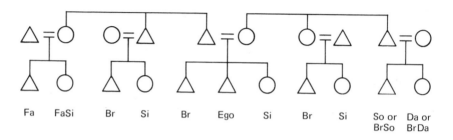

| Fa | FaSi | Br | Si | Br | Ego | Si | Br | Si | So or BrSo | Da or BrDa |

In the *Omaha* type system, parallel cousins are referred to by the same terms used to refer to brother and sister, while both patrilateral and matrilateral cross-cousins have distinctive terms. Father's sister's son is referred to by the term used to refer to son or sister's son, and father's sister's daughter by the term used to refer to daughter or sister's daughter; on the other hand, mother's brother's son is referred to as mother's brother and mother's brother's daughter as mother. Omaha kinship systems are usually associated with patrilineal descent groups.

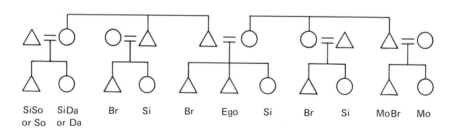

| SiSo or So | SiDa or Da | Br | Si | Br | Ego | Si | Br | Si | MoBr | Mo |

16. What type of kinship terminology for first cousins is employed?
   1. Hawaiian
   2. Eskimo
   3. Sudanese
   4. Iroquois
   5. Crow
   6. Omaha

Most ethnographies include kinship terms, either in a table or on a diagram. If the diagram is similar to the type used in this section, a direct comparison with the above types can be made. If the diagram is not similar or a table of terms is given, the terms can be written below an unlabeled diagram of the above type and then the comparison can be made. If the kinship terminological system being studied does not fit one of the six types, the student needs to make a judgment as to whether it could be derived from or is a variation of one of the six types. If he cannot make a judgment, the system cannot be classified and it should be recorded in full detail. (For practice in the analysis of kinship systems the exercises in Schusky's *Manual for Kinship Analysis* [1965] are recommended.)

Iroquois kinship terminology for first cousins is employed by the Yąnomamö (Chagnon 1968:56):

Their kinship system is called the "bifurcate merging" type with "Iroquois" cousin terms (see Glossary). Within each generation, all the males of one lineage call each other "brother," and all the women call each other "sister." Males of lineage X call males of lineage Y "brother-in-law" and are eligible to marry their sisters. In fact, the males of lineage X call the females of lineage Y "wife" *whether or not they marry them.* This is likewise true for the males of lineage Y with respect to the females of lineage X. [Italics in the original.]

The Chagnon glossary contains a definition of "Iroquois kinship terms" which is essentially the same as the definition given in this section.

Gamst provides a complete list of kinship terms for the Qemant (1969:73). The appropriate terms can be written below an unlabeled diagram.

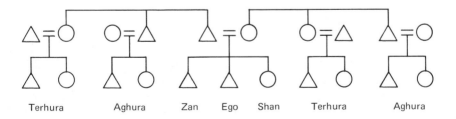

Terhura   Aghura   Zan   Ego   Shan   Terhura   Aghura

Comparison of this diagram with each of the six diagrams fails to reveal a complete correspondence. It is most similar, however, to the diagram illustrating Eskimo terminology, since brother and sister are differentiated from both types of cousins. In fact, Gamst classifies the system as Eskimo (1969:72):

> According to the widely used Spier-Murdock classification, based principally upon terms for cousins, kin terms of the Qemant are of the Eskimo type. The Yankees also have the Eskimo system in which terms for siblings are distinct from terms for cousins.

Although the kinship terminology can be described as Eskimo, it should be noted that parents' brothers' children (Aghura) are differentiated from parents' sisters' children (Terhura).

CHAPTER 4

Polity
and Warfare

Anthropologists interested in the political aspects of any culture must concern themselves with four factors. First, they must distinguish polities and ascertain the manner in which these political units are distributed on the earth's surface. There is always this spatial aspect. Such units may be large or small—both in population size and in amount of territory occupied. Second, they must analyze the organizational structure of the polities in terms of their component units and the types of leaders which head these units. Special attention must be paid to the political leaders who head the polities. Third, they must describe the means by which conflicts within the political units are resolved and the manner in which decisions made by leaders are enforced. Such a description constitutes an analysis of the legal systems of the polities. Fourth, anthropologists must study the relationships between polities in order to provide a complete description of the political aspects of any culture. These relationships include diplomacy and warfare (Bohannan 1963:266–267).

Political Communities

The local groups in most cultures are organized into territorial units known as political communities. The organization derives from the existence of a leader or leaders who perform tasks which are important to the members of the local groups composing the political community. Sometimes the local groups are not organized into larger units, but are themselves political communities. The functions performed by the leaders of political communities may include ceremonial, economic, and political tasks. Ceremonial tasks may include the blessing of crops and animals, serving as an intermediary between men and gods, or simply being a symbol of territorial unity. Economic tasks may include serving as the redistribution agent for a nonlocal allocative center or the overseer of an economic system based upon market exchange (see "Economy of Culture" on p. 32). Political tasks may include the adjudication of disputes, the enforcement of decisions, and the initiation and direction of warfare. None of these tasks is necessarily performed by the leader of a political community. In order to recognize territorial units and their leaders in ethnographic accounts it is necessary to have a definition of political community. Such a definition has been provided by Raoul Naroll (1964:268): "A group of people whose membership is defined in terms of occupancy of a common territory and who have an official with the special function of announcing group decisions —a function exercised at least once a year." Although this is Naroll's definition of a "territorial team," it is preferable for semantic reasons to call territorial units *political communities*—it is difficult to conceptualize large states as teams—and to call the officials or leaders of such territorial units *political leaders*. A political community is a maximal territorial unit; that is, it is not included within a larger unit.

Both political communities and cultures have a spatial dimension. A political community is composed of local groups organized into a territorial unit under the direction of a political leader, while a culture is composed of local groups whose members share the same culture and speak the same language. Since both kinds of units are composed of local groups, it is possible to find local groups of the same culture in several political communities or to find local groups of different cultures in the same political community. These two possibilities give rise to two basically different types of situations which are illustrated in Figure 2. First, one or more political communities occur within a single culture. Since each political community is composed of local groups of the same culture, each political community within the culture is culturally homogeneous. A consequence of this homogeneity is that the members of the local groups, whether they are in the same political community or not, can communicate with each other since they speak the same language. Most of the cultures of the world, except in regions with complex political systems, are divided into several political communities. Second, a single political community includes local groups from two or more cultures. Thus the political community is culturally heterogeneous. A consequence of this heterogeneity is that the members of the local groups which are culturally different cannot communicate with each other, since they speak different languages. Bilingualism or the use of a lingua franca in most instances appears to overcome only partially the difficulty in communication. Heterogeneous political communities are usually found only in regions of complex political systems.

Situation 1

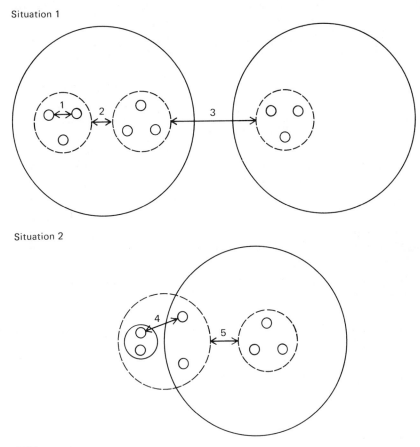

Situation 2

KEY:

Circles
Small circles represent local groups
Broken-line circles represent political communities
Solid-line circles represent cultures

Double-headed arrows (⟵⟶)
1 relationships between local groups within the same culture
2 relationships between political communities within the same culture
3 relationships between political communities within different cultures
4 relationships between culturally different local groups within the same
   political community
5 relationships between a culturally heterogeneous and a homogeneous political
   community

Figure 2. Diagram of Basic Concepts—II

　　When two or more political communities occur within a culture and the culture is adjacent to one or more other cultures, three types of inter-group relationships can be distinguished. First, relationships will exist between the local groups within each political community. These relationships may include economic reciprocity, joint military operations, use of land in common, joint cooperation on ceremonial occasions, and membership in the same clans or phratries. These intra-political community relationships are overseen by the leader of the political community, and in some political communities he has the power to intercede and adjudicate disputes arising out of these relationships. Where adjudication occurs law exists. Second, relationships will exist between the political communities within the culture. Third, relationships will exist between the political communities which are within two adjacent cultures. The relationships between political communities, whether they are culturally the same or not, are different from the relationships which occur within political communities, since there is not a single political leader who can oversee the relationships. Diplomacy, warfare, and trade are the major kinds of inter-political community relationships. Members of the same culture, although they are in different political communities, have the same cultural perspective with which to deal with problems and conflicts arising out of inter-political community relationships. Members of different cultures will deal with such problems and conflicts from the perspective of their own cultures, for there is usually no commonly accepted way of handling such matters (Campbell and LeVine 1961:82–108). Thus it is important to distinguish the relationships between political communities which are culturally the same from the relationships between political communities which are culturally different.

　　When a single political community includes local groups from two or more cultures and the political community is adjacent to other political communities, two types of intergroup relationships can be distinguished. First, relationships will exist between local groups which are culturally the same and those which are culturally different. Since the members of culturally different local groups do not speak the same language, problems arising between such local groups are difficult for the political leader to resolve. That is, heterogeneous political communities are characterized by conflicts which develop out of "race relations." Resolution of the problems and conflicts is difficult, not only because of the communication problem, but also because the political leader is usually a member of one of the two contending cultures. Second, relationships will exist between the political community and adjacent political communities. The type of inter-political community relationships will probably be the same whether or not the neighboring political communities are culturally homogeneous or hetero-geneous, since cultural differences exist between the political communities. The only situations in which cultural differences might not be of importance would be when the dominant culture in both political communities is the same.

17. Are the political communities culturally homogeneous or heterogeneous?
    1. If homogeneous, how many political communities are there in the culture?
    2. If heterogeneous, how many cultures are included in the political community?

Naroll's definition of a territorial team should be used to distinguish political communities. In counting the number of political communities within a culture, only maximal territorial units should be enumerated. By maximal is meant that the unit with its political leader is not included within a larger unit. Maximal territorial units or political communities may contain subunits within them which have their own leaders. In some cultures, particularly those whose political systems are not complex, there may be a large number of political communities. The number of political communities may total in the hundreds—if each local group within the culture is a maximal territorial unit. When a culture of this type is being analyzed, it may be necessary to estimate the number of political communities, provided the ethnographer does not furnish a figure. In addition, if the information is available, the size—in terms of population—of each political community should be recorded. If there are a large number of political communities in the culture, the average size can be determined by dividing the number of political communities into the population size of the culture.

In many instances it is difficult to distinguish political communities, since many cultures have been conquered and absorbed into modern nations and the leaders of the constituent political communities have been incorporated into the political structures of the nations. Schapera's definition is an attempt to deal with this problem (1956:8): "By a 'political community' I mean a group of people organized into a single unit managing its affairs independently of external control (except that exercised nowadays by European governments)." Probably the best solution to the problem is to utilize information dealing with the culture which pertains to a period before the culture lost its political autonomy. For some cultures, such as those of highland New Guinea, that period is now; for others it is the eighteenth or nineteenth century. This period between the time that Europeans first discovered and observed a culture and the time that the culture's political communities were absorbed into the conquering nation is known as the *ethnographic present.* If information pertaining to the ethnographic present is utilized to distinguish political communities, the date or approximate time level to which the information applies should be recorded.

Each Yąnomamö village is a political community (Chagnon 1968: 101):

> Whether the ties between neighboring villages will be one of blood, marriage exchange, reciprocal feasting, or casual trading depends on a large number of factors, particularly on village size, current warfare situation with respect to more distant groups, and the precise historical ties between the neighboring villages. Whatever the nature of the ties between neighbors, each strives to maintain its sovereignty and independence from the others.

The political communities are culturally homogeneous. Chagnon estimates the number of Yąnomamö villages at 125 (see Question 7 for quotation).

For hundreds of years (since A.D. 1300) the Qemant have been absorbed into larger political communities—first, the "medieval Abyssinian feudal state," today, the modern nation of Ethiopia (Gamst 1969:15–16). It is thus impossible to describe the Qemant political community as it existed prior to its conquest. For this reason Ethiopia has been selected as the political community. Therefore, the questions in this chapter, "Polity and Warfare," will be answered from this perspective. Where possible, however, the relationship of the Qemant to this larger political unit will be examined.

Ethiopia is a heterogeneous political community which includes seventy or more cultures (Gamst 1969:5–6):

> The affinities of the Qemant to their neighbors in Ethiopia, an area of 450,000 square miles populated by an estimated 22,000,000 people divided into seventy or more language groups, are of interest. The northern and north-central part of highland Ethiopia, once called Abyssinia, is the region in which field research was conducted. It is inhabited by three major groups which together are sometimes called Abyssinians. They are: the Amhara, who number about 5,000,000 and are politically dominant; the Tegre, numbering about 1,500,000, and the Agaw, who are the original inhabitants of most of the region, with a population of about 250,000, and the group to which the Qemant belong. These three peoples are racially one and have many common cultural roots as well, in spite of the fact that the first two groups speak Semitic languages and the third group speaks dialects belonging to the central branch of the Cushitic languages. . . .
> All Agaw speak either mutually intelligible or nearly mutually intelligible dialects of the Agaw language, and almost all Agaw are bilingual, also speaking Amharic or Tegrenya.

Political System

The territorial organization of a political community may form a system consisting of a series of hierarchical levels. Although some political communities are composed of only one local group, most are composed of numerous local groups. Sometimes these local groups are organized into territorial units within the political community. These territorial units are called districts. In some political communities the districts are organized into larger territorial units called provinces. Local groups, districts, and provinces—like the political community itself—are headed by political leaders. There is one hierarchical level if the political community is composed of one local group, two levels if it is composed of two or more local groups, three levels if it is composed of districts, and four levels if it is composed of provinces. These levels form a system in that the leaders at each level, except for the head of the political community, are subordinate to a leader at a higher level. Political communities differ one from the other in terms of the number of hierarchical levels composing their political systems. The more levels there are to a political system, the more complex it is. Thus the number of levels provides a measure of political complexity. The greater the number of hierarchical levels the greater the complexity of the political community.

Two basic types of political communities were delineated in the previous section: those which are culturally homogeneous and those which are culturally heterogeneous. Homogeneous political communities are composed of local groups of the same culture. If a political community consists of only one local group, it of course will be culturally homogeneous. Thus the political systems of culturally homogeneous political communities will range in complexity from one to several hierarchical levels. Culturally heterogeneous political communities are composed of local groups of different cultures. Since there must be two or more local groups in a heterogeneous political community, there must also be at least two hierarchical levels present. Thus the political systems of culturally heterogeneous political communities will range in complexity from two to several hierarchical levels. Since heterogeneous political communities cannot consist of only one level, it follows on a logical basis that heterogeneous political communities will have complex political systems. There is also an empirical reason why the political systems of heterogeneous political communities are complex. The conquest of local groups by culturally different local groups not only produces, by definition, heterogeneous political communities, but it also creates a series of hierarchical levels, since it is necessary for the leaders of the conquering local groups to superimpose an administrative organization upon the conquered local groups. Since a complex political system is a means of territorially organizing conquered local groups, political communities with such political systems are likely to be culturally heterogeneous. (Of course, local groups of the same culture may also be organized into a complex political system through conquest.)

18. How many hierarchical levels are there in the political system?

If each local group in the culture is a maximal territorial unit, there is only one level to the political system of each political community. If there are several local groups in a political community, there are two hierarchical levels to the political system. If local groups are organized into districts with district leaders, there are three hierarchical levels. A lineage and clan system, if the lineages are local groups and the clans are districts, will form a three-level political system. If districts are organized into provinces with district and province leaders, a political system with four hierarchical levels exists. A lineage, clan, and phratry system—if the lineages are local groups, the clans districts, and the provinces phratries—constitutes a four-level political system. It is also possible to find complex political systems with more than four hierarchical levels. If such a system is being analyzed the exact number of levels should be recorded.

Since each Yąnomamö village or local group is a maximal territorial unit, there is only one hierarchical level to the political system of each political community (see Question 17).

There are five hierarchical levels in the political system of Ethiopia (Gamst 1969:21):

> Ethiopia has five levels of government administration: (1) the nation or Empire, (2) the province or Governor Generalate (*tekelay gazat*), (3) the subprovince (*awraja*), (4) the sub-subprovince (*warada*), and (5) the sub-sub-subprovince (*meketel warada*).

The Qemant are divided between two subprovinces (Gamst 1969:21):

> One-half of the Qemant are in the Gondar *awraja*, which is administered from the town of Gondar, and the other half are in the Chelga *awraja*, which is administered from the village of Aykel, near the eastern boundary of this *awraja*.

Political Leaders

The leaders of political communities or maximal territorial units vary greatly in the tasks, either ceremonial, economic, or political, which they perform. Thus one way of classifying political leaders would be in terms of the tasks which they perform for the members of their political communities. Another way to classify leaders would be in terms of how they succeeded to political office: is succession based on hereditary principles, is there a formal election, does informal consensus occur, or is the position seized by the strongest individual? Leaders vary also in two other attributes: degree of formality and degree of power. In terms of degrees of formality, a leader may be almost indistinguishable from other adult males in the culture. He may dress no differently, his demeanor may be the same, and he may not be referred to by any special name. At the other extreme, the leader may be so formal that he is believed to be a deity or an earthly incarnation of a deity. Leaders likewise vary greatly in terms of their degree of power. On one hand, a leader may be so limited in power that he has no other function except announcing group decisions; and on the other hand, a leader may have such great power that he can arbitrarily put individuals to death. These two variables or attributes—degree of formality and degree of power—can be used together to construct a typology for classifying political leaders. Such a classification will be followed here.

The above two variables are used by Leopold Pospisil to derive a scheme for classifying types of political leaders, or as he calls them, authorities (1958:260–261):

> These different attributes allow the authorities to be classified as different types. For our purposes we may be interested in two attributes: formality and extent of power. . . .
>
> To give some tentative definitions of our extremes, we may say this: by formal authority is meant an individual (or individuals) with his (or their) role, rights, duties, and activities defined by custom and/or law. . . . The informal authority, on the other hand, has no ceremonial importance and little public emphasis. . . . His rights, duties, and procedures are not defined by law or custom.
>
> A limited authority is acquired by a procedure which is controlled by the society. Approval by the majority of the members of the society is necessary, or nomination by another person with relatively greater authority must take place. . . . An absolute authority is different in many respects. His power is not limited by someone else. The subordination of his followers is emphasized in personal contacts. . . .
>
> By measuring the two variables discussed above, we should be able to place each authority in a definite position that indicates his qualities within the two ranges. An authority then will be defined by the following possible combination of the two measured attributes and their negatives: formal and absolute, informal and absolute, formal and limited, or informal and limited. . . .

Pospisil ends his development of the typology at this point. It is possible, however, to proceed further and to label each of his four combinations with a pertinent term. Four types of political leaders are listed in the following chart along with their defining attributes:

Types of Political Leaders	Degree of Formality	Degree of Power
King	formal	absolute
Dictator	informal	absolute
Chief	formal	limited
Headman	informal	limited

Thus a typology of four different types of political leaders has been constructed. Each type is defined in terms of the degree of formality and the degree of power of the political leader. Political communities headed by leaders with absolute power (kings and dictators) are known as *states,* and political communities headed by leaders with limited power (chiefs and headmen) are considered to be stateless (Fortes and Evans-Pritchard 1940).

These terms—*king, dictator, chief, headman*—can be used not only to classify the leaders of political communities, but also to classify the leaders of subunits within political communities. The leaders of subsidiary local groups, districts, and provinces will probably have less formality and power than the leader of the political community. Many different combinations of leaders can occur, the combinations depending in part upon the number of hierarchical levels within the maximal territorial unit. Some likely combinations are as follows: king, chiefs, chiefs, headmen; king, chiefs, headmen; chief, headmen, headmen; king and chiefs; chief and headmen. Dictators will rarely be found, since in most cases a political leader who has absolute power and who is not a formal leader will rapidly attempt to formalize the position which he has just seized or created by bestowing titles upon himself, by wearing special clothing, by claiming certain social prerogatives, and possibly even by claiming to have been divinely chosen. Political scientists would say such a leader is attempting to legitimize his position.

19.   What type of political leader is present?
  1.   king
  2.   dictator
  3.   chief
  4.   headman

If there is more than one hierarchical level in the political community, the type of leader of each subunit should also be recorded.

In the classification of political leaders several difficulties are likely to arise. In the first place, the definitions of formal, informal, limited, and absolute are definitions of the extreme ends of two variables or continua.

If a political leader fits somewhere near the middle on either variable, it may be difficult to make a decision as to whether his position is formal or informal or whether his power is limited or absolute. If the difficulty arises, a decision should be made nevertheless, and a statement describing the basis for the decision should be recorded. Another difficulty in classifying political leaders stems from the indiscriminant use in some ethnographies of two of the above terms. The terms chief and headman are sometimes applied to any leader without regard for the tasks or functions which he performs. Thus, for example, the term chief may be used to describe an informal leader, while the term headman may be used to describe a formal leader. This difficulty can be avoided by ignoring the terms employed in the ethnography and by classifying the leader according to his tasks and functions. Once the degree of formality and power of the leader have been established, the appropriate term for the type of political leader can be ascertained from the above chart. Yet another difficulty in classifying political leaders may arise if there are several leaders or a council occupying the top position in the political community. They may be kings, dictators, chiefs, or headmen, or a council of the same. If multiple political leaders exist this should be noted.

The political leader of each Yąnomamö political community is a headman because he is an informal authority and has a limited degree of power (Chagnon 1968:96):

> Kąobawä has definite responsibilities as the headman and is occasionally called upon by the nature of the situation to exercise his authority. He is usually distinguishable in the village as a man of some authority only for the duration of the incident that calls forth his leadership capacity. After the incident is over, he goes about his own business like the other men in the group. But even then, he sets an example for the others, particularly in his ambitions to produce large quantities of food for his family and for the guests he must entertain. Most of the time he leads only by example and the others follow if it pleases them to do so. They can ignore his example if they wish, but most of the people turn to him when a difficult situation arises.

The present political leader of Ethiopia is Emperor Haile Sellassie I (Gamst 1969:16). Although specific information is not given in the ethnography, it can be inferred from descriptions of the relationship of the Qemant to the central government that the political leader has great power and has formal authority (Gamst 1969:16,20–22,57,119–122). He can be classified as a king.

The Qemant have their own leaders, all of whom have limited power (Gamst 1969:3):

> The indigenous political structure of the Qemant . . . has three levels: councils of elders on the lowest level, higher and lower priests in intermediate positions, and the *wambar*, the arch politicoreligious leader, at the apex. The wambar acknowledges the secular sovereignty of the Amhara administrators who have social positions and roles within an ascending hierarchy of authority constituting what might be termed a feudal system.

The *wambar* and the priests are formal authorities (Gamst 1969:39–43), and thus can be classified as chiefs (see Question 26). Elders, on the other hand, may be either formal or informal leaders (Gamst 1969:58):

> Councils of elders are the basic units of authority among the Qemant. The councils are democratic assemblies composed of males who are "old enough to have gray hair" and who usually have a moderate amount of prestige. Elders who do most of the debating and have the greatest voice in making decisions are those who have undergone the rite of *kasa*, marking transition to the esteemed status of venerable elder. This special status signifies marked closeness to Mezgana (God). Although the rite of kasa is not required for all elders, the councils of elders are closely integrated with the religion.

Thus some elders can be classified as chiefs, others as headmen.

Legal System

In every political community there are conflicts between individual members of the same or of different local groups which create ruptures in intra-political community relationships. These conflicts between individuals are referred to as *trouble cases* by anthropologists who study "primitive law." In many political communities the political leader has the power to intercede and adjudicate disputes. Sometimes this is done by a leader of a subunit within the political community or by a special official whose function is to adjudicate trouble cases. The leaders of some political communities have so little power that they cannot intercede and settle disputes; in these political communities ruptures in intra-political community relationships persist. If the rupture is serious, such as a feud resulting from a homicide, the political community may fragment and form two political communities. Kings and dictators, by definition, have the power to intercede and adjudicate disputes. Chiefs and headmen—although their power is limited—may have sufficient power to settle disputes. Thus any type of political leader may be able to resolve conflicts between individuals.

If trouble cases are resolved by political leaders (or by authorities acting in their stead), a situation exists in which law can develop. Two elements, in addition to "official authority," must be present for law to exist: "privileged force" and "regularity" (Hoebel 1954:28). The authority must be able to back his decision with physical force, and the use of this force must be deemed appropriate by the members of the political community. The decision must be applied with regularity in similar trouble cases. If an authority does not intend for his decision to be applicable to other trouble cases, nor does he employ decisions made earlier by himself or by other authorities in resolving the trouble case, the settlment of the trouble case is not legal. That is to say, the decision is political, not legal. If these three elements are involved in the settlement of some disputes, law is present in the political community. If authorities do not have the power to apply physical coercion to enforce decisions and do not apply decisions with regularity, law does not exist.

Two types of legal sanctions may be applied by an authority: restitutive and penal. A restitutive sanction is a requirement that one individual (the defendant) must make payment to the other individual (the plaintiff) in the dispute. Payment is usually in the form of animals, material goods, money, or some other type of wealth. If payment is not made, the authority may use physical force. The use of a restitutive sanction defines a legal case as being an example of the *law of private delicts*. Modern jurisprudence would classify such actions as cases of civil law. Actions treated as private delicts include homicide, wounding, theft, adultery, and failure to pay debts. A penal sanction, on the other hand, is a punishment inflicted upon an individual who is responsible for violating a rule of conduct. Penal sanctions include incarceration, exile, beating, and execution. These sanctions come into effect when the local group or the political community as a whole has become outraged over the behavior of an individual or when the decisions or commands of authorities have been disobeyed. Such situations are not, strictly speaking, trouble cases unless the offended local group or the authority is viewed as a party in the dispute. Nevertheless, "cases" in which penal sanctions are employed are legal since the three defining elements of law are present. The use of a penal sanction defines a legal case as being an example of the *law of public delicts*. Western law would define such actions as cases of criminal law. Actions treated as public delicts include incest, sorcery, sacrilege (Radcliffe-Brown 1952:212–219). From the point of view of judicial process it should be noted that if the defendant in a trouble case does not make restitution, he has disobeyed the decision of the authority; if such disobedience leads to the application of a penal sanction, the case becomes transferred from the realm of private law to the realm of public law. Thus penal sanctions reinforce restitutive sanctions. Since, by definition, penal sanctions (that is, the legal use of physical force) must be present for law to exist within a political community, the law of public delicts is always present if the law of private delicts is present. The converse is not true, since penal sanctions do not depend upon restitutive sanctions.

20. What types of law are present?
   1. law absent
   2. law of private delicts (based upon restitutive sanctions)
   3. law of public delicts (based upon penal sanctions)

The first task facing a person undertaking an analysis of the legal system of a political community is to identify the political leader and any other authorities who make decisions, decisions which are often attempts to resolve trouble cases. If penal sanctions are regularly employed to punish individuals who break rules of conduct or to enforce restitutive sanctions, law exists—in particular the law of public delicts. If restitutive sanctions are used by authorities in resolving trouble cases and these sanctions are reinforced by penal sanctions, then the law of private delicts is also present. If authorities cannot enforce a restitution requirement imposed upon one of the individuals in a dispute, neither restitutive nor penal sanctions are present; and therefore law is not present. Thus a political community may be without law, it may have public law only, or it may have both public and private law. Private law alone does not occur.

The position taken here differs from that taken by some anthropologists who study "primitive law." Hoebel (1954) and Pospisil (1958), for example, interpret the key concepts—official authority, privileged force, and regularity—so broadly that at least some trouble cases in any political community are classified as legal cases. (For a criticism of their position consult Fried [1967:90–94,141–153].) Regularity requires that there be multiple cases involving the same decision; penal sanctions must actually be applied at times for there to be evidence of privileged force; and an authority must be an official, not a forceful individual who usurps the privilege of settling trouble cases. All three elements must be present in the settlement of some disputes for law to exist in a political community.

———————

The Yąnomamö have no law. The official authority—the headman— seemingly does not have the right of privileged force, nor is there apparently any regularity in the settling of conflicts. The following trouble case involving the ethnographer indicates that Kąobawä, the headman, was unable to adjudicate disputes (Chagnon 1968:68):

> On one occasion a young man stole my flashlight and gave it to
> Shiimima, a younger brother to Kąobawä, but already a mature adult.
> I asked Kąobawä to help me get it back. After a day or so I asked him
> if he had gotten my flashlight back from Shiimima, whereupon he re-

plied: "I have spoken to him about it. He will return it if he sees fit. I cannot order him to do so because he is already fierce."

In another trouble case, the headman could possibly be exercising privileged force, but there is no indication that similar trouble cases would be handled in the same manner (Chagnon 1968:120):

One of the young men took the wife of another because she was allegedly being mistreated by him. This resulted in a brutal club fight that involved almost every man in the village. The fight escalated to jabbing with the sharpened ends of the clubs when the husband of the woman in question was speared by his rival and wounded. The headman of the village . . . had been attempting to keep the fighting restricted to clubs. When the husband's rival speared his opponent, the headman went into a rage and speared him in turn, running his own sharpened club completely through the young man's body. He died when they tried to remove the weapon. The wife was then given back to her legitimate husband, who punished her by cutting both her ears off with his machete.
The kinsmen of the dead man were then ordered to leave the village before there was further bloodshed.

The Qemant legal system is embedded in the administrative and judicial system of Ethiopia. Thus the wambar's decisions are enforced by higher Ethiopian authorities (see Question 22). For this reason penal sanctions can be said to be present. The wambar also has the power to impose ostracism. It is not clear, however, from the following passage whether this sanction involves physical removal from Qemantland. If it does not, ostracism is not a penal sanction (Gamst 1969:63):

The wambar preserves Qemant mores with awesome punishments that reach beyond the grave and bar the way to heaven. Curses and ostracism are the ultimate punishments handed out by a wambar, and they are ordinarily levied only if someone challenges his authority. For example, if a person does not abide by a wambar's decision, or if he violates a major religious rule, such as marrying outside Qemant religious laws, he is ostracized. Ostracism is complete and final and continues after death. An ostracized person receives no funeral and no rite of passage into heaven.

Restitutive sanctions are also present. In homicide cases blood money may be paid (see Question 22 for quotation). The amount of restitution may be as high as Eth. $1000 (Gamst 1969:63).

Since penal and restitutive sanctions occur, both the law of public delicts and the law of private delicts are present. This would be true for both Ethiopia and the Qemant.

Military Organizations

A military organization is the means by which a political leader defends his political community from enemy attacks. It may also be used internally by the political leader to enforce the law and to carry out penal sanctions. Military organizations can range in size from small raiding parties composed of several warriors to large standing armies composed of hundreds of thousands of men (Mead 1964:270). Armed combat, which is fighting with weapons, is performed by military organizations. If there is more than one military organization within a political community and these military organizations engage each other in armed combat, this is considered feuding or civil war, depending upon the scope of the conflict. Warfare (excluding civil war) is defined as armed combat between political communities. When the political communities within the same culture engage in warfare, this is considered to be internal war. When warfare occurs between political communities which are not within the same culture, this is referred to as external war. These concepts relating to the activities of military organizations are discussed in this and the next two sections; the relationships among these major concepts are graphically illustrated in Figure 3. Concepts dealing with aspects of military and political organization are represented by circles, and types of armed combat between military and political organizations are shown by double-headed arrows (Otterbein 1968b).

Military organizations, which can be viewed as a particular type of social organization, engage in armed combat in order to obtain certain goals. They differ, however, from other organizations in that the goals or objectives they pursue are usually directed at military organizations in other political communities. The goals of war include subjugation and tribute, land, plunder, trophies and honors, defense, and revenge (see "Causes of War" on p. 91). All these objectives are carried out at the expense of other political communities. The military organization which is the winner of the armed combat is more likely to achieve its goals than is the defeated military organization. The outcome of an armed combat between two military organizations will depend upon the efficiency of their military practices. A victorious military organization makes a political community militarily successful and increases its likelihood of survival in inter-political community conflicts (Otterbein 1970a).

The warriors composing a military organization may be either professionals or nonprofessionals. Professionals, in contrast to nonprofessionals, devote a substantial part of their time during their early adulthood to intensive training, which may involve not only practice in the use of weapons but also practice in performing maneuvers. They may be members

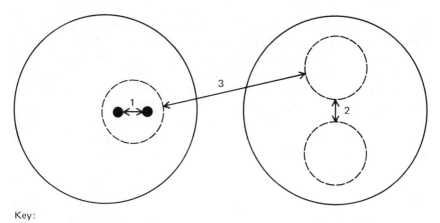

Key:

    Circles
Solid circles represent military organizations
Broken-line circles represent political communities
Solid-line circles represent cultures

    Double-headed arrows (⟵⟶)
1   feuding
2   internal war
3   external war

Figure 3.   Diagram of Basic Concepts—III

of age-grades, military societies, or standing armies, or they may serve as mercenaries employed for a specific purpose. Political communities with age-grades, military societies, and standing armies are considered to have military organizations composed solely of professionals. Political communities which employ mercenaries to lead, train, or assist untrained warriors are considered to have both professionals and nonprofessionals in their military organizations. If all members of a military organization are warriors who have not had intensive training in the art of war, the military organization is considered to be composed solely of nonprofessionals. If both professional and nonprofessional warriors are absent, there is of course no military organization. A recent cross-cultural study of war examined the military practices of fifty cultures. It was found that nine political communities had military organizations composed of professionals, thirteen had military organizations which included both professionals and nonprofessionals, twenty-four had military organizations composed of nonprofessionals, and only four had no military organizations (Otterbein 1970a). Thus one is most likely to find military organizations composed of nonprofessional warriors. On the other hand, one rarely finds a culture which does not have a military organization.

The fact that few political communities do not have military organizations raises the fundamental question: Why do most political communities have military organizations? The answer seems to be that if a political community is to have contact with other political communities and yet to remain a social entity, it needs to have the means to defend itself from the attacks of neighbors and to retaliate if the attacks have been successfully made against them. The four political communities without military organizations, mentioned above, are all found in isolated locations. Their members are descendants of groups which had been driven from other areas and which had taken refuge on an island, in arctic wasteland, or on the top of a mountain. Relocated in an area where they were protected by their isolation, they no longer found it necessary to maintain a military organization. Thus a political community which does not have a military organization capable of defending it will probably be annihilated and absorbed into other political communities unless it is able to flee and protect itself, not by arms, but by hiding in an isolated area. A further indication that a military organization is a necessity, if a political community is to persist through time, is to be found in the fact that defense and revenge are universal causes of war. Several studies have shown that all known military organizations go to war at some time or another for defense and revenge (Otterbein 1970a; Naroll 1966; Wright 1942).

21. What type of military organization is present?
   1. a military organization is absent
   2. a military organization composed of professional warriors
   3. a military organization composed of both professional and non-professional warriors
   4. a military organization composed of nonprofessional warriors

If all the military personnel in the political community are either members of age-grades, military societies, standing armies, or mercenary units, the type of military organization present is composed solely of professional warriors. On the other hand, if none of the warriors has had intensive training in the art of war, the military organization is composed entirely of nonprofessional warriors. It is also possible that the political community will have a military organization composed of both professional and nonprofessional warriors.

It is clear from Chagnon's detailed description of Yąnomamö warfare that their military organizations were not composed of age-grades, military societies, standing armies, or mercenaries. As the following quotation indicates, the training of a warrior was an informal, on-the-spot process (1968:130–132):

The raiders always develop a strategy for attacking the unwary enemy. They usually split into two or more groups and agree to meet later at a predetermined location at some point between their own village and the enemy's. These smaller groups must contain at least four men, six, if possible. This is so because the raiders retreat in a pattern. While the others flee, two men will lie in ambush, shooting any pursuers that might follow. They, in turn, flee, while their comrades lie in ambush to shoot at their pursuers. If there are novices in the raiding party, the older men will conduct mock raids, showing them how they are to participate. A grass dummy or soft log is frequently employed in this, as was the case in the *wayu itou* held in the village the day before the raiders left. Particularly young men will be positioned in the marching party somewhere in the middle of the single file of raiders so they will not be the first ones to be exposed to danger should the raiders themselves be ambushed. These young men will also be permitted to retreat first. Damowä had a twelve-year-old son when he was killed. This boy, Matarawä, was recruited into the raiding party to give him an opportunity to avenge his father's death. The older men made sure he would be exposed to minimum danger, as this was his first raid.

Hence, it can be concluded that Yąnomamö military organizations are composed of nonprofessionals.

Although explicit information is lacking, it can be inferred from Ethiopian history that the military organization is composed of professional warriors (see Question 24 for quotation). The Qemant do not have their own military organization, but they have served with distinction in the Ethiopian army (Gamst 1969:21,81,105,109).

Feuding

Feuding is a type of armed combat within a political community in which if a homicide occurs, the kin of the deceased take revenge through killing the offender or a close relative of his. Such armed combats are usually initiated by a small group of men, relatives of the deceased, who lie in ambush and attack the unsuspecting victim who is often alone and has little chance of escape. The ambushers are of necessity sufficiently armed and organized that the group which they form can be referred to as a military organization; that is, a sufficient degree of organization must prevail if the warriors are to arrange the ambush in secret, to remain silently in hiding, and to spring the attack at the appropriate moment. These small-scale military organizations are fraternal interest groups. They are usually composed of nonprofessionals. It has been shown by van Velzen and van Wetering (1960) that fraternal interest groups, which are power groups composed of related males, resort to aggression when the interests of their members are threatened. Such groups can come into existence either through the operation of a patrilocal (or virilocal) residence rule, since patrilocal residence produces households in which related males are living together, or through the practice of polygyny, since polygyny usually produces a situation in which men will have a number of unmarried sons living with them. If residence practices and marriage rules result in the scattering of related males over a large area, it will be difficult for them to support each other's interests.

A cross-cultural study of feuding has demonstrated that fraternal interest groups—as measured by patrilocal residence and polygyny—lead to feuding. One would think that in a complex political system the political leader would intercede and prevent the relatives of the victim from taking blood revenge, either by use of a judicial procedure or by persuading the relatives of the deceased to accept some form of compensation for their loss. Contrary to expectations, the study shows that this does not necessarily occur. If fraternal interest groups were present, feuding was found to be frequent in cultures whose political communities had complex political systems consisting of more than one hierarchical level. Since the political leaders who head these political communities are likely to be kings and dictators (and perhaps chiefs with some degree of power, although it be limited), this is surprising. The study does show, however, that political communities with complex political systems do not have feuding if they frequently engage in warfare. Presumably these leaders use their power to intervene to prevent the development of feuding only when the political community is threatened by war or is engaged in war. In political communities with simple political systems consisting of only one hierarchical level, warfare does not diminish the frequency of feuding. Since the leaders of such political communities are chiefs and headmen with limited power, they are unable to intervene to prevent feuding. In other words, in a political community there is an official who can, if he has sufficient power, and will, if he perceives that the inter-political community situation demands it, intervene between the feuding fraternal interest groups. Since it is only in complex political systems that political leaders have sufficient power— power which they may choose to exercise only under demanding circumstances—to control the activities of the warriors in their political communities, it is only in complex political systems which are engaged in war that one finds that the feuding of fraternal interest groups is curtailed (Otterbein and Otterbein 1965; Otterbein 1968b).

Homicide cases are handled by political communities in three different ways: (1) Feuding does not occur if there is a formal judicial procedure for punishing the offender or if homicides are always settled through compensation. (Of course, feuding is not likely to arise if homicides rarely occur.) The trouble cases arising out of homicides are legally adjudicated if the political leader or an authority imposes a restitutive or penal sanction upon the party responsible for the homicide. (2) Feuding with compensation occurs if the relatives of the deceased sometimes accept compensation in lieu of blood revenge. (3) Feuding without compensation occurs if the relatives of the deceased are expected to take revenge through killing the offender or any close relative of his. If feuding invariably follows a homicide or if compensation need not be accepted by the relatives of the deceased, the trouble cases resulting from homicides are not legally adjudicated. In many cultures accidental as well as deliberate homicide can trigger feuding. In other words, the offended fraternal interest group does not take into account the intentions of the killer. However, in those cultures which have feuding with compensation, the intention of the killer may determine whether compensation is accepted. That is, if the relatives of the deceased are convinced that the homicide was accidental, they may be willing to accept compensation. On the other hand, in those cultures which have feuding without compensation, accidental homicide will probably lead to feuding.

22. Is feuding present?
  1. absent
  2. feuding with compensation
  3. feuding without compensation

Feuding is absent if there is a formal judicial procedure for punishing killers or if the account states that homicides rarely occur. Feuding occurs if the kin of the deceased take revenge through killing the offender or a close relative of his. If restitution in the form of animals, material goods, money, or some other type of wealth is sometimes offered by the relatives of the killer and is sometimes accepted by the relatives of the deceased, feuding with compensation occurs. If restitution is never offered and never accepted, feuding without compensation occurs. If the ethnography—and it is highly unlikely—provides statistical data on homicides and how they are resolved, this information should be recorded.

Feuding without compensation may occur among the Yąnomamö, and when it does it leads to village fissioning, with each segment becoming a separate political community (Chagnon 1968:40–41):

> By the time a village approaches 100 to 150 people, such fights over women are so frequent that the group elects to fission rather than

attempt to keep an uneasy internal peace. Although a larger village has an advantage in terms of its capacity to raid other groups and is better able to defend itself from raids, the internal fights often lead to killings within the group. Then, there is no alternative but for one of the factions to leave. Its members may anticipate a situation like this and begin making a new garden long before the fighting becomes violent enough to lead to deaths, for a fight can develop unexpectedly and result immediately in bloodshed. The guilty faction must then seek refuge in the village of an ally until it can establish its own garden. Usually, however, the larger group fissions while its members are on relatively peaceable terms, and the two resulting villages remain in the same general area so that they can reunite when raids threaten them.

For a specific example of fissioning, see Question 20.

When conflicts over women arise, it is usually between men of different local descent groups (see Question 13) belonging to the same patrilineage. Two or possibly more local descent groups will break away from the village, taking with them two or more local descent groups (with whom they intermarry) from another lineage (Chagnon 1968:70–71).

Although killings and counterkillings occur among the Qemant, feuding is absent. Gamst decribes homicides at length (1969:63–64):

> The most serious judicial matter to reach a wambar is a killing. Qemant law does not recognize accidental death or manslaughter; to take another person's life is to murder him. The dictum of "an eye for an eye" is Qemant law, and the penalty for taking another's life is for the killer to lose his own life at the hands of the dead man's kin. The killer has only one recourse: He may pay blood money to the family of the person he has killed. . . .
>
> If the family of the killer cannot come to an agreement with the family of the deceased through councils or other intermediaries, the wambar takes up the problem. If agreement is reached by both parties on the amount of indemnity, an oral contract is made with the help of the wambar or council of elders. This contract is then presented by both parties to the Amhara officials, who levy an additional fine upon the guilty person and confiscate any weapon used in the killing. In this way the Amhara validate Qemant judgments in cases of homicide. After the contract is fulfilled and the fine is paid, the killer cannot be punished further. . . .
>
> Today, if a judgment of blood indemnity is disputed, the case may be referred to the Amhara judges and administrators. If the Amhara officials do not settle the case, as happens occasionally, the kin of the deceased take the life of the killer. In keeping with the idea of blood vengeance, an endless chain of vendetta may then ensue, but this rarely happens. The policy of the Ethiopian government is to try to punish for killings, thus preventing vendettas.

There are three reasons for concluding that feuding is absent: (1) there is a formal judicial procedure for punishing the offender; (2) it is the killer himself who is killed, not one of his kin (elsewhere, however, Gamst [1969:70] states otherwise [see Question 14 for quotation]); and (3) vendettas "rarely" occur.

Warfare

Warfare, which is defined as armed combat between political communities, is conducted by military organizations. If the political communities are culturally the same, the armed combat is classified as internal war. But if the political communities are culturally different, the armed combat is external war (see Figure 3 on p. 83). Two types of external war can be distinguished: a political community can either attack (offensive external war) or be attacked by (defensive external war) a culturally different political community. The military organizations which carry out the armed combat are apt to be fraternal interest groups. As was pointed out in the previous section, if the members of such a military organization make an attack upon someone who is a member of their own political community, they are engaged in feuding or the initiation of a feud. If the next day these warriors ambush a member of another political community, they are engaged in war. Thus, fraternal interest groups, employing ambushing tactics, can be responsible for both feuding and warfare. It has been shown in a cross-cultural study of internal war that fraternal interest groups lead to frequent internal war. This apparently occurs because most cultures with fraternal interest groups probably contain a large number of such military organizations because of the large number of localized kinship groups in the constituent political communities. The presence of a large number of small-scale military organizations creates the strong likelihood that internal war will be frequent. Presumably because of the greater distance between most political communities which are in different cultures, fraternal interest groups do not produce either the offensive or the defensive type of external war (Otterbein 1968a; Otterbein 1968b).

The frequency of internal war can be classified as either "continual," "frequent," "infrequent," or "never." The two types of external war can also be classified in the same manner. However, for the sake of brevity, external war and its frequency will not be discussed. It is necessary to classify the frequency of internal war on a four-point scale, since it is nearly impossible—even for an ethnographer in the field—to record the number of different attacks which the political communities within a culture make upon each other in a particular period of time. Most ethnographies include only general statements concerning the frequency of war. For any particular culture and its constituent political communities, the frequency of internal war can be classified as "continual" if the ethnographic source states that warfare is or was a constant state of affairs within the culture. Constant can be interpreted to mean that warfare occurs every year. Internal war is "frequent" if the source states that although the political communities within the culture frequently fought with each other, periods of peace occasionally occurred. An indication that periods of peace occur would be a statement that warfare is not an annual affair. Internal war is "infrequent" if warfare is described as uncommon or rare. And finally, the frequency of internal war can be classified as "never" if warfare is described as nonexistent or if there are no military organizations in the culture.

23. If there is more than one political community within the culture, how frequently do they war with each other?
   1. continually
   2. frequently
   3. infrequently
   4. never

The first problem to be faced in attempting to ascertain the frequency of internal war is to make certain that there is more than one political community within the culture. This has already been established if Question 17 dealing with political communities has been answered. If there is only one political community in the culture or the political community is culturally heterogeneous, internal war as defined in this section cannot occur. Another problem is to find sufficient information dealing with the culture before it was militarily defeated and absorbed into a conquering state, probably a European nation. Lack of sufficient information is one reason why most ethnographies contain only general statements concerning the frequency of war. Since the ethnographic present for some cultures occurred as much as 200 years ago, detailed information is often lacking on warfare.

Yąnomamö political communities continually war with each other. Chagnon is one of the few ethnographers who has actually witnessed warfare while undertaking fieldwork (Chagnon 1968:40):

The village of Patanowä-teri, for example, has over 200 people. It was being raided actively by about a dozen different groups while I conducted my fieldwork, groups that raided it about twenty-five times in a period of fifteen months.

Since Ethiopia is a heterogeneous political community (that is, there are not distinct political communities within a particular culture), this topic and question are not applicable to the situation.

Causes of War

Wars occur when military organizations do battle in order to obtain certain goals. These goals may vary from war to war, and they may change over time. Thus for the military organizations of a political community there will probably be several goals of war. At a given period in the history of a political community—if sufficient data are available—the order of the importance of the goals can probably be ascertained. The political leader of the political community may determine the goals and send the military organizations to war in order to achieve these goals, or the leaders of the military may make the decision as to which goals will be pursued. Thus it can be argued that wars are caused by the decisions of men as members of organizations, whether they be military organizations or political systems. There are six reasons for going to war: subjugation and tribute, land, plunder, trophies and honors, revenge, and defense (Otterbein 1970a).

Some social scientists have argued that states, which are political communities headed by kings or dictators, go to war for subjugation and tribute. On the other hand, political communities headed by chiefs and headmen go to war for economic, social, and defensive reasons. Of the fifty cultures in a cross-cultural study of war, ten consisted of political communities which were states. The states of seven of these cultures went to war for political objectives—namely, subjugation and tribute. Only two cultures had political communities which were not states, but which nevertheless went to war for subjugation and tribute. These cultures were composed of political communities with strong leaders (Otterbein 1970a). This almost exclusive association between states and political objectives can be explained by two conditions which must exist for subjugation and tribute to occur. First, the victorious political community must have a complex political system consisting of several hierarchical levels if it is to have the capability of incorporating conquered peoples into its political system. Moreover, the political community must have a political leader with a great deal of power who can superimpose himself and the members of his political community upon vanquished peoples. Such a leader is to be found only in states and some political communities with complex political systems. Second, even though the political machinery for subordination is present, subordination must be advantageous to the victors—advantageous in the sense that the skills possessed by the conquered peoples and the products they produce are of value to the victorious political community. If the conquered peoples are coerced into contributing some of the products which they produce to the leaders of the victorious political community, tribute is being paid. Thus states, subjugation, and tribute form a complex which is found again and again throughout the world.

The other five reasons for going to war are also likely to be pursued at one time or another by the military organizations of states. They also constitute the major reasons stateless political communities go to war. An important economic reason for attacking other political communities is to capture land by defeating and driving back or killing the inhabitants. The land may be used for fields, hunting, or grazing. Another goal of war, primarily economic, is to obtain plunder. Plunder, in addition to animals, material goods, money, and other forms of wealth, includes captives for slaves, hostages, adoption, or sacrifice. Trophies and honors are social or prestige goals. Military organizations and political communities often go to war, just as individual warriors do, to obtain honors. Victory in armed combat may be the sole reason for going to war. The capturing of trophies, which are cherished items usually of little economic value, is another way of obtaining prestige. Revenge—the desire to even the score—is another reason military organizations go to war. Retaliation for the killing of a member of one's political community is often a major reason for revenge. And the final reason military organizations engage in war is defense—the organized attempt by a group of armed men to defend from enemy attacks their own lives, the lives of their families, their property and homesteads, and their political community.

24. For what reasons does the military organization go to war?
   1. subjugation and tribute
   2. land
   3. plunder
   4. trophies and honors
   5. revenge
   6. defense

   If there is more than one reason for going to war, each reason should be indicated. If the ethnographer explicitly states the order of importance, his ranking should be recorded. If such a statement is not given, the student will have to judge the order of importance from the emphasis given to the various causes of war by the ethnographer. If a judgement cannot be made, the order in the ethnography in which the causes are listed or discussed can be tentatively accepted as representing the order of importance. Of course if the political community does not have a military organization, this question is irrelevant.

———————

   Yąnomamö military organizations go to war for revenge, defense, and plunder (in the form of women) (Chagnon 1968:123):

> Most wars are merely a prolongation of earlier hostilities, stimulated by revenge motives. The first causes of hostilities are usually sorcery, murders, or club fights over women in which someone is badly injured

or killed. Occasionally, food theft involving related villages also precipi-
tates raiding. . . .

Although few raids are initiated solely with the intention of capturing women, this is always a desired side benefit. A few wars, however, are started with the intention of abducting women.

The military organization of Ethiopia has gone to war for the follow-ing reasons: defense, revenge, land, and subjugation and tribute (Gamst 1969:16):

In the 1870s and 1880s Emperor Johannes IV defended Abyssinia against Egypt and then against the Dervishes of the Mahdi in the Sudan. Emperor Menelik II (1889–1913) turned back European intrusion at the battle of Adwa (1896), in which the Italians were defeated and their plans for colonization were shattered. Menelik II established the capital at Addis Ababa, conquered lands to the south of Abyssinia, and intro-duced elements of western industrial urban technology. Under Menelik's reign, Abyssinia was transformed and expanded into a larger, more modern nation named Ethiopia.

Change in Ethiopia continues at a faster rate under the present Emperor, Haile Sellassie I. Ethiopia experienced occupation by mechan-ized Italian military forces from 1936 to 1941, in the early years of the Emperor's reign.

CHAPTER 5

World View
and Life Cycle

Anthropologists who are interested in the development of the personality of individuals within a culture focus not only upon the typical life cycle of both men and women in the culture, but also upon that part of culture which is referred to as the people's world view. According to Robert Redfield (1952:30), world view is that "outlook upon the universe that is characteristic of a people. . . . It is the picture the members of a society have of the properties and characters upon their stage of action." Supernatural beings, religious practitioners, magic, and sorcery are among the more important aspects of a people's world view. They are aspects which directly impinge upon the maturing individual. Various situations and events also influence individuals from the time of birth until death. To focus upon the common practices and customs which influence individuals at different stages of their lives is to focus upon the typical life cycle of individuals within a particular culture. Birth customs (such as the post-partum sex taboo), the games children and adults play, adolescent initiation rites, and artistic pursuits are some of the practices and events which are likely to compose the life cycle.

Supernatural Beings

Most peoples do not distinguish between the natural and the supernatural worlds. For them the beings and spirits—which anthropologists classify as belonging to the supernatural realm—are as much a part of their everyday world as are their own relatives and neighbors. Supernatural beings or spirits are believed to be real—real in the sense that they exist and can influence and be influenced by human beings. Supernatural beings are personified; that is, they have personal identities, and they often have names. "They have purposes and intentions of their own as well as the power to achieve their objectives" (Swanson 1960:7). They are usually immortal, they may be invisible, and they reside in particular locations either on the earth or above or below it. Although anthropologists consider supernatural beings or spirits to be unreal (in fact, the ethnographer in the field identifies spirits on the basis of their lack of reality), it must be emphasized again that supernatural beings are real to the people who believe in them. Belief in supernatural beings is called *animism*, a term introduced to anthropology by Edward B. Tylor in his famous book *Primitive Culture* (1958; orig. 1871).

Of the various types of supernatural beings in which a people believe, a high god, if present, is usually considered to be the most important of their supernatural beings. A *high god* is a supernatural being who created the universe and/or is the ultimate governor of the universe. In some instances the high god may have created other supernatural beings who in turn produced the universe. Some high gods, after they created the universe, became inactive and no longer play any part in human affairs. Other high gods play an active part in the affairs of humans. Some active high gods give specific support to human morality; that is, the gods reward or punish people in accordance with their treatment of relatives and neighbors. The belief in a high god is not rare among the peoples studied by anthropologists. In a cross-cultural study of the origins of religious beliefs, Swanson (1960:65) found that nineteen out of thirty-nine cultures had a belief in a high god (data were missing for eleven cultures). Swanson did discover, however, that the belief in such a supernatural being was associated with social and political complexity. That is, cultures with lineage and clan systems and/or with political communities with several hierarchical levels are more likely to have a belief in a high god than are cultures which are structurally less complex (Swanson 1960:55–81).

Many cultures with a high god also have superior gods. These supernatural beings are often under the direction of a high god who on occasion may need to intercede to keep order among them. Superior gods personify human activities such as hunting, farming, going to war, and making love. Each god controls all individuals who engage in any aspect of those activities associated with the god. They are not spirits who control particular individuals or places. *Superior gods* are supernatural beings "who control all phases of one or more, but not all, human activities" (Swanson 1960: 210). The belief in superior gods is found among a majority of cultures. In the above mentioned cross-cultural study, Swanson (1960:87) found that twenty-nine out of forty-nine cultures had a belief in one or more superior gods. Furthermore, he discovered—as one would expect—that superior gods were characteristic of cultures that had part-time and full-time specialists, since superior gods are the personification of human activities, including various types of specialties (Swanson 1960:82–96).

In virtually all cultures human beings are believed to have a soul or spirit which persists after death. Spirits of the dead may go to a hereafter, or they may remain somewhere on earth. In either case they may or may not play an active part in the affairs of the living. When the spirits of the dead influence their living relatives, ancestral spirits are present in the culture. Thus *ancestral spirits* are supernatural beings who are spirits of the dead and who play some role in the affairs of their living relatives. Some ancestral spirits aid or punish their descendants. This may be to enforce morality, or to force the living to pay homage or to make sacrifices to them. In some cultures nothing that the living can do will prevent ancestral spirits from inflicting hardships upon them. In other cultures individuals may invoke their deceased relatives to aid them in their earthly pursuits, such as hunting or harming an enemy. The belief in ancestral spirits is widely spread: Swanson (1960:216) found that thirty-three out of forty-nine cultures had beliefs in active ancestral spirits. Moreover, he discovered that ancestral spirits were associated with organized kinship groups. When descent groups—which are ancestor-oriented groups—such as lineages, ambilineages, clans, and phratries are present in a culture there exists an important bond between the living and the dead; that is, social relationships exist between members of the descent group and the deceased ancestral members of the group (Swanson 1960:97–108).

In addition to high gods, superior gods, and ancestral spirits, there are supernatural beings or spirits present in many cultures which are non-human in origin, although they may have human attributes. These *non-human spirits* are supernatural beings who control particular individuals or places. In some cultures an individual may through various means acquire a guardian spirit who protects him from evil or harm. The spirit may be an animal with human attributes who is the ancestor of a particular species. Many cultures have a large number of nonhuman spirits who are associated with particular geographical locations. These spirits often dwell in lakes, rivers, prominent rocks, and mountains. Sometimes they can be invoked to assist in human activities, such as hunting and fishing. At other times they must be placated or they are apt to molest passers by. They, like guardian spirits, may be animal ancestors, or they may be animal-like creatures who have both human and animal attributes.

25. In what types of supernatural beings do the people believe?
   1. a high god
   2. superior gods
   3. ancestral spirits
   4. nonhuman spirits

Since all four types of supernatural beings are commonly found in the cultures studied by anthropologists, it is to be expected that more than one type of supernatural being will be present. If there are superior gods, each should be identified and the number recorded. The number of nonhuman spirits, if there are any, will probably be so great that it would be nearly impossible to enumerate them all.

For those interested in the classification of religious belief systems, the following scheme can be used: Monotheism is usually defined as the belief in one god. Therefore, if a high god is present, but superior gods are not, the religious belief system can be classified as *monotheistic*. On the other hand, polytheism is usually defined as the belief in more than one god. Therefore, if superior gods are present, with or without a high god being present, the religious belief system can be classified as *polytheistic*.

Chagnon provides a lengthy description of Yanomamö supernatural beings. Since there is no mention of a high god when the origin of the universe is being described, it can be concluded that a high god is absent. Superior gods, however, are in abundance (Chagnon 1968:45):

> The first beings cannot be accounted for. The Yanomamö simply presume that the cosmos originated with these people. Most of them, and there were many, had a specific function, such as creating a useful plant or object. They figure prominently in mythology. Many of them bear the names of plants and animals that are important to the Yanomamö economy, and the first beings are considered to be the spirits of these.

Some of these superior gods are: Bore (first to have plantains, the headman of the first things), Iwä or alligator (first to have fire), Haya or deer, Öra or jaguar, Omauwä (sends hiccups, sickness, and epidemics to the Yanomamö), Periboriwä or Spirit of the Moon (wounded, the blood changed into men as it hit the earth), and Wadawadariwä (directs the souls of the deceased to different parts of the hereafter).

When a Yanomamö dies part of his soul goes to the hereafter, another part becomes a malevolent spirit (Chagnon 1968:48–49):

> Yanomamö concepts of the soul are elaborate and complicated. The true or real portion of living man is his "will" or "self" (*buhii*). At death, this changes into a *no borebö* and travels from this layer to *hedu*, the place above where the souls of the departed continue to exist in an ethereal state, much in the same fashion as do the people on earth: gardening, hunting, and practicing magic.
>
> Another portion of the soul, the *no uhudi* or *bore*, is released at cremation. This part of the soul remains on earth and wanders about in

the jungle. The children who die always change into this, as they do not have the *no borebö* portion that goes to *hedu*: It must be acquired. . . . Apart from this, one is born with an *uhudi* (*bore*), which is invariably released at cremation and wanders eternally in the jungle after death. Some of these wandering *uhudi* are malevolent and attack travelers in the jungle at night. When they do so, they use sticks and clubs.

Finally, each individual has a *noreshi*. This is a dual concept: One has a *noreshi* within his being, a sort of spirit or portion of the soul, and, in addition, an animal that lives in the jungle and corresponds to his soul. The *noreshi* animals are inherited patrilineally for men and matrilineally for women.

These malevolent spirits should not be classified as ancestral spirits since they do not play a role in the affairs of their living relatives. Other nonhuman spirits are the *hekura* (see Question 26) and Wadoriwä, the spirit of the wind, who blows leaves off the roofs of houses (Chagnon 1968:28).

The Qemant believe in all four types of supernatural beings. The high god is *Mezgana*, the sky god (Gamst 1969:34–35):

According to Qemant, their God is male and resides in the sky. He is not different in reality from the ancient Agaw Sky God and somewhat resembles the Hebrew God worshipped by the Hebrao-pagan Falasha Agaw. Belief in the ancient Sky God is one of the principal traits that distinguishes the Qemant from their neighbors, who abhor such a marked manifestation of paganism. . . .

Qemant believe Mezgana is omnipresent, omnipotent, and omniscient, and that everything was created by Him; therefore, He has the right to destroy everything. He is an anthropomorphic God; Qemant say, "Mezgana looks like man."

A superior god is Saytan (Gamst 1969:39):

Saytan is the essence of all that is evil. Qemant, Amhara, and Falasha uniformly conceive of Saytan as being very black and horrible-looking, having human or animal form, and possessing great powers, including the ability to cause thunder and lightning.

Qemant believe in deities which Gamst calls angels since they are equated with Hebrao-Christian angels (1969:37). Since their functions are not described, it is not possible to ascertain whether they control any human activities.

Ancestral spirits, each of whom has his own sacred grove, are active in human affairs (Gamst 1969:35):

Although members of the Qemant priesthood sometimes contact Mezgana directly, they usually reach Him through intermediary culture heroes called *qedus. Qedus* means "saint" and "holy" and applies to the spirits of dead human beings who are culture heroes. . . .
Holy culture heroes of the Qemant are, for the most part, the ancestral heads of the clans in the Keber moiety, the more important of the two Qemant moieties. Other culture heroes include ancestors of these heads and certain wives of the ancestors.

Some of these ancestral spirits fit into a pantheon, described in mythology, which provides the Qemant with an unwritten history which they use to validate present-day claims to land and to determine their place among other peoples (Gamst 1969:35–37).

Non-human spirits are in abundance (Gamst 1969:38):

They [genii loci] are minor deities who have strong control over limited areas, usually part or the whole of a single community. A genius loci is called a qole and is referred to by the name of the place where it is venerated. . . .

Elsewhere Gamst states that (1969:28):

Sites of qole worship are in high places, almost always on hilltops or on the edge of an escarpment. They are usually marked by a single tall tree or a prominent rock or pinnacle.

Some persons have personal spirits which may possess them (Gamst 1969:45):

Any person may have a zar as well as other personal spirits, although most people do not have a zar, and those who do sometimes find that the spirit might not be present for months or years. Zars may be either male or female and are often of the same sex as the human beings with whom they are associated. Although usually benevolent or neutral, when "neglected," zars may become malevolent, causing disease or other misfortune. A zar can possess a person, causing uncontrolled motion and speech.

On the other hand, all persons have guardian spirits (Gamst 1969:49):

Although not everyone has a zar, everyone is said to have a guardian spirit, generally referred to as *yeqole* [my (guardian) spirit]. . . .
Personal qoles rarely possess people, but should they turn malevolent

or otherwise become bothersome, a shaman may be consulted to handle
them.

There are also disease spirits (Gamst 1969:51):

> While personal spirits may bring illness to a person, specific spirits of
> disease may cause illness of epidemic proportions to befall an entire
> community. These spirits of disease apparently have no other function.

Religious Practitioners

Religious practitioners are intermediaries between men and supernatural beings. In some cultures each individual may be able to deal directly
with some or all of the supernatural beings. In other cultures there are
specialists who serve as intermediaries for individuals, local groups, or
political communities. These specialists, in their role as intermediaries, perform certain tasks or functions for both men and supernatural beings. On
one hand, they may communicate the wishes of the members of their local
group or political community to certain powerful gods, and on the other
hand, they may interpret the wishes of the gods to the local group or
political community. Different techniques are employed in performing these
functions. Divination may be used to foretell future events; ceremonies,
rituals, and offerings may be made to please the supernatural beings;
prayer may be used to čajole gods and spirits; and magic may be practiced
to manipulate and coerce them. Because these functions are important to
both the beings who are part of the supernatural world and to the men who
live on earth, religious practitioners are usually important members of the
local group. In small political communities they may even be headmen. In
larger political communities they may exercise more influence than the
political leader.

Two types of religious practitioners are distinguished by anthropologists: shamans and priests. Both are specialists, the former part-time,
the latter full-time. The *shaman*, who may earn his subsistence like every
other man, devotes part of his time to serving as an intermediary, usually
for individuals. He often works alone, since he is not usually a member of
an organization composed of shamans. He may have learned to be a shaman
from an older shaman, or he may have gained his abilities from direct
contact with supernatural beings. Sometimes he has a guardian spirit who
visits him while he is in a trance state. One of the most common reasons
individuals employ shamans—who are often expensive—is to determine
the cause of an illness and to cure it. Divination may be used to seek the
cause, and magic may be used to cure it. Since many peoples do not dis-

tinguish between illnesses of natural origin and those of supernatural origin (caused perhaps by sorcery or malevolent spirits), shamans frequently serve as medicine men for all types of illnesses.

The *priest*, who normally is supported by the community, devotes nearly all of his time to serving as an intermediary, usually for his local group or political community. He is often a member of a religious organization, which has provided him with special training. Years of training may be necessary before full-fledged membership in the priesthood is granted. Membership in the priesthood legitimizes his position as a religious practitioner. On important occasions he and other priests may participate in ceremonies and rituals which are believed to be vitally necessary by the members of the local group or political community. These ceremonies, which express group sentiments and beliefs and which are performed in the presence of most members of the local group, are known as *rites of intensification* (Chapple and Coon 1942:397–415). In carrying out his duties, the priest may serve as an interpreter for the gods. If the gods are satisfied that their wishes are being carried out, they will assist men in their daily activities. Sometimes the priest attempts to persuade important supernatural beings to help. Prayers, offerings, and sacrifices are the means which he uses (Honigmann 1959:636–638; Lessa and Vogt 1958:410–411).

26. What types of religious practitioners are present?
   1. absent
   2. shamans
   3. priests

Religious practitioners may not be present, but if they are, then it is necessary to determine whether they are shamans or priests. Both types, however, may be present. Although shamans and priests differ in a number of respects, the difference which should be used to distinguish between these two types of religious practitioners is their degree of specialization. If they are part-time specialists, they are shamans; if they are full-time specialists, they are priests.

Shamans, but not priests, are the Yąnomamö religious practitioners (Chagnon 1968:52):

The nature of the relationship between man and spirit is largely one of hostility. The shamans, by and large, spend most of their time casting charms on enemies and enjoining their own personal demons to prevent harm from befalling the local people. Magic and curing are intimately bound up in shamanism, the practitioner devoting his efforts to causing and curing sickness.

The demons that the shamans contact are *hekura*, very tiny humanoid beings that dwell on rocks and mountains. Particularly successful shamans can control these demons to such an extent that the *hekura* will come and live inside the chest of the shaman. Each shaman solicits the aid of numerous *hekura* and attempts to lure them into his body.

Men who want to become shamans (*shabori*) go through a simple rite of fasting and chastity. They sit before their houses, use only a few trails, eat very little, and spend most of their time in a contemplative stupor brought about by hunger and drugs. After several days of this, the initiate has entered the world of the *shabori*, and can practice his skill. Each village has as many *shabori* as there are men who wish to enter this status: probably half of the men in each village are shamans.

The Qemant have both shamans and priests. Gamst describes a particular shaman (1969:44):

Ayo, who is Erada's brother and fifty-four years of age, is like most Qemant a plowman, but he also serves as a part-time religious practitioner. Ayo deals with zars and other personal spirits, performing the role of *balazar* (master of the zar), usually in a special house of his homestead about 1000 feet from that of Erada. . . . In anthropological classification, the balazar is a shaman, one who acquires his supernatural power and his social position from his ability to contact directly animistic (spiritual) beings. These are usually minor spirits for whom the shaman serves as a medium or "mouthpiece" when the spirit takes possession of him. Shamans of the Qemant and neighboring peoples are additionally often leaders of cults addressed to personal spirits.

The priesthood is described at length (Gamst 1969:39–40,43):

Priests . . . are organized into a hierarchy and must learn formalized ritual patterns in order to act as middlemen for communication between humans and the beings of their animistic world. . . .
He [the wambar] officiates at major ceremonies where priests perform rituals attempting to manipulate nature through supplication of members of the pantheon. The wambar makes life secure for the Qemant by praying to regulate the weather, to end disease or other personal misfortune, to eradicate dangerous wild animals, and to punish transgressors of laws. His most important act is praying for the dead during the rite of passage which follows funerals, to assure their entry into heaven. . . .
Under the wambar are two levels of priests. The higher, called *kamazana*, is elected from the Keber moiety, and the lower, *abayegariya*, is elected from the Yetanti moiety. Like the wambar, the priests must come from certain lineages in certain clans that have traditionally

supplied the personnel for these religious positions. After a man has been elected to priesthood by the community, he is taken by the people to the wambar, who blesses him and confirms his appointment. . . .

Each community has at least one higher priest and one lower priest who work together in all ceremonies. . . .

Priests are remunerated with bars of salt for their services in performing the ritual in various rites of passage, rain-regulating ceremonies, and curing ceremonies such as the one with the livestock. The major source of priestly income, however, comes from labor which adult males in each community must supply to the local priests.

Magic

The practice of magic involves three elements: the practitioner (who may or may not be a shaman or priest), the practical aim or end to be achieved, and the magical formula itself. When an individual has an objective to achieve which cannot be coped with by ordinary means or which requires the assistance of a supernatural being, he may either practice magic himself or employ someone, possibly a shaman, to perform the magic. The practical ends for which magic is often used cover a wide range of objectives. They include objectives which can be classified as protective in that they prevent harm to the individual or cure him of illness. Other objectives can be classified as productive; they include the desire for a successful hunt, an abundant crop, ample rains, and even success in courtship and love making. Still other objectives are destructive; they include the desire to harm or destroy one's rivals or enemies (see "Sorcery" on p. 108).

There are three aspects to the magical formula itself. First, the things used—the instruments or *medicines*. The ingredients used in magic are often difficult to obtain and to prepare. They may be difficult to obtain because they are rare or because they must be taken from or have been in contact with the being—either human or supernatural—which one wishes to influence. Second, the things done—the *rite*. The preparation of the medicines, the manner in which medicines are combined, and the placement of the medicines either on or near that which is to be influenced constitutes the rite. Third, the things spoken—the *spell*. The verbal element in magic may consist of a series of words and phrases which are fixed and invariable, or it may be simply an overt expression of the practitioner's desires. The medicines, the rite, and the spell are almost always present in any magical formula. Their relative importance, however, may vary from formula to formula and from culture to culture. For example, most cultures which are located on the African continent south of the Sahara Desert or which originated in Negro Africa place major importance on the medicines employed. On the other hand, many cultures in the Pacific Ocean region place great emphasis on the spell (Firth 1958:125–128).

Although the belief in magic appears irrational to the rational mind, there are a number of positive functions or effects which may stem from the practice of magic. In cultures in which magic is extensively practiced, most individuals are fearful that any suspicious or harmful act attributed to them will result in the threatened individual attempting to harm them, possibly through magic. Thus magic functions to promote social control by deterring many people from cheating and stealing (Otterbein 1965a). Moreover, the belief in magic may in itself deter individuals from practicing magic, since magic can be considered a suspicious or harmful act if its occurrence is discovered. The practice of magic may play an important role in technological and subsistence pursuits. It provides positive and negative sanctions, thus insuring that tasks are properly performed. Furthermore, magic creates confidence in the face of uncertainty. The belief in magic provides a theory about the nature of the world. Failure, misfortune, and death can be attributed to the practice of harmful magic. The practice of magic may also provide emotional relief for an individual who believes that he has been wronged, if he himself practices countermagic. The practitioner can vent his rage and satisfy his desire for revenge.

James George Frazer, in his famous twelve-volume work *The Golden Bough*, distinguished between two types of magic (1911:52):

> If we analyze the principles of thought on which magic is based, they will probably be found to resolve themselves into two: first, that like produces like, or that an effect resembles its cause; and, second, that things which have once been in contact with each other continue to act on each other at a distance after the physical contact has been severed. The former principle may be called the "Law of Similarity," the latter the "Law of Contact or Contagion." From the first of these principles, namely the Law of Similarity, the magician [practitioner] infers that he can produce any effect he desires merely by imitating it: from the second he infers that whatever he does to a material object will affect equally the person with whom the object was once in contact, whether it formed part of his body or not.

Magic based on the law of similarity is called *homeopathic magic*, and magic based on the law of contagion is called *contagious magic*.

27. What types of magic are practiced?
  1. homeopathic magic
  2. contagious magic

Since magic is almost universally found among the peoples of the world, it is unlikely that any culture studied by an anthropologist will be found not to have magic. In order to classify the magic practiced by the members of a culture, it is necessary to analyze a series of magical formulae. Particular attention should be given to the medicines. If they resemble that which is to be influenced, the law of similarity is being employed. Two common examples are the sticking of needles into a doll in order to injure or kill the individual which the doll resembles and the pouring of water onto the ground in order to produce rain. If the medicine has been in contact with a person, such as his clothing, or was once a part of the person's body, such as hair or nail clippings, the law of contagion is being employed. On occasion, both the law of similarity and the law of contagion may be present in the magical formula. For example, the victim's nail clippings are placed inside the doll with the needles stuck in it. In fact, rarely will the law of contagion be found to be solely present in a magical formula. Thus of the magical formulae analyzed, some may be classifiable as examples of homeopathic magic and others may be classifiable as examples of both homeopathic and contagious magic. If only formulae which can be classified as homeopathic magic are found in the culture, the only type of magic practiced is homeopathic. If homeopathic magic is present and some other formulae can be classified as both homeopathic and contagious magic, then both homeopathic and contagious magic are practiced by the members of a culture.

Homeopathic magic, using plant medicines, is practiced by all Yąnomamö (Chagnon 1968:37–38):

> Most of the magical plants are associated with benevolent or at least nonmischievous functions. "Female charms" (*sua härö*), for example, are used by men to make women more receptive to sexual advances. . . . Another magical plant is cultivated by the women. Its leaves are thrown on the men when they have club fights because it allegedly keeps their tempers under control and prevents the fight from escalating to shooting. Still other plants are cultivated to insure that male or female children grow up to be healthy adults, a different plant being associated with each sex.
> Some of the plants are cultivated for malevolent purposes, such as causing the women in enemy villages to have miscarriages or pains in the back when they are pregnant, while other plants allegedly cure the same evils.

Homeopathic magic is also practiced by shamans. As the following account indicates, medicines are not a part of the formula (Chagnon 1968:52):

> If he is curing someone, he chants before the house of the patient, rubs him, massages him, and draws the evil spirit causing the sickness to

some extremity, such as an arm or leg. Then he sucks or pulls the spirit out and carries it away from the sick person, either vomiting it out or throwing it away, depending on how he extracted it originally. The Yąnomamö do not employ medicines made from plants or animals. Consequently, they rely exclusively on the cures that the *shabori* effect, fighting supernatural ills with supernatural medicine.

Contagious magic appears to be absent. No direct evidence is provided. Moreover, *hekura*—not magic—are used by shamans to harm others.

Although Gamst describes Qemant magic, none of his examples can be analyzed as either homeopathic or contagious magic. Some magic is used to protect animals and crops (Gamst 1969:54):

> To protect cattle, the trailing edges of their ears are notched while the cattle are young; to protect crops, skulls of cattle on poles, or several poles made from limbs or small trees from which the bark has been peeled, are placed upright in the fields. No reason could be found for these actions except that they were "known to be effective."

Magic is employed to protect oneself (Gamst 1969:54):

> To safeguard oneself against black magic, Qemant, Falasha, and Amhara wear amulets as protection against malevolent spirits and other forms of evil. Amulets are charms with protective functions and are made by magicians. In the Qemant area, amulets consist of small pieces of inscribed parchment placed in a small leather case that is worn around the neck on a cord.

Magic is also used to injure people (Gamst 1969:54–55):

> When sorcerers (black magicians) practice their dark arts, they may at times use empirical means, such as drugs or physical acts of destruction, but usually they rely upon their incantatory spells, to which objects of medicine have been adroitly added. This latter method has been used against Erada. For example, when one antagonist wishes misfortune to befall Erada, he purchases some "medicine" eggs from a sorcerer. Chanting and gesturing over the eggs, the sorcerer guarantees to bring misfortune to anyone upon whose premises the foul eggs are buried. When darkness falls and Erada's dogs are asleep, the antagonist buries the eggs near Erada's homestead.

One must conclude that magic is present even though the examples given cannot be analyzed in terms of the principles of thought on which they are based.

Sorcery

The use of magic, supernatural beings, or other supernatural powers to deliberately attempt to harm or destroy another person is known as *sorcery*. An individual who uses these supernatural means to destroy others is known as a *sorcerer*. As pointed out in the previous section, one means of injuring or killing another person is through the practice of contagious magic. The presence of contagious magic in a culture, although in itself not evidence that sorcery is practiced, nevertheless provides a strong indication that sorcery occurs. Another means of practicing sorcery is to invoke a supernatural being, such as a guardian spirit or an ancestral spirit, to assist one in harming an enemy. Sometimes an individual has the ability to utilize unseen supernatural powers to bring about the destruction of another individual. The sorcerer accomplishes this by willing or performing a psychic act. In less formal terms, he is said to put a curse or an evil eye upon a person. Since magic, malevolent spirits, and unseen supernatural powers can be used to cause injury, illness, or death to individuals, there are many cultures in which sicknesses and misfortunes are attributed to the practice of sorcery. In such cultures an individual who has become ill or who has had a series of tragedies employs a shaman to diagnose and cure his illness or difficulties. The shaman may be able to not only identify the sorcerer, but also to practice magic which will counteract the malevolent attack. If the shaman is a man of great ability, he may be able—usually for a handsome reward—to use magic or other supernatural means to inflict harm upon the sorcerer. In other words, he becomes a sorcerer himself. Battles or duels between sorcerers are sometimes described in ethnographic accounts.

Sorcery, like magic, functions to promote social control by deterring many individuals from cheating, stealing, and harming others (see "Magic" on p. 105). In cultures in which sorcery is practiced an individual believes that any harmful acts which he does may be discovered, perhaps through divination or other magical means. Once the acts are discovered he believes that he himself will be in danger of bodily harm—often in the form of a sorcerer's attack. Thus individuals are deterred from harmful acts and even from practicing sorcery itself. Those cultures whose political communities are headed by political leaders with little power (that is, headmen and chiefs) and whose legal systems are poorly developed (possibly penal sanctions are absent) are deficient in formal mechanisms of social control. Such political communities must rely upon informal mechanisms of social control such as sorcery. B. B. Whiting (1950) in a cross-cultural study of sorcery tested the theory that sorcery can serve to maintain order in cultures which lack formal mechanisms of social control. She discovered that sorcery was important—that is, it was given as a cause of illness in the ethnographic accounts—in those cultures in which no authority or political leader possessed sufficient power to settle disputes or punish offenses. In her terminology "superordinate control" was absent. On the other hand, sorcery was found to be unimportant in those cultures whose political communities were characterized by superordinate control.

In many cultures in which sorcery is practiced the social control aspect may, during times of great misfortunes, cease to function in a manner which stabilizes interpersonal relationships. Normally the belief in and the occasional practice of sorcery prevent many individuals from engaging in acts harmful to others. When crises arise and misfortunes occur to the local group, those members most affected seek explanations for what has happened or is happening. If these individuals believe in sorcery, they may conclude that their misfortunes are the result of an increase in sorcerers or an increase in the activities of known sorcerers. The individuals suffering the mishaps may become so infuriated that they will attack and kill people known as sorcerers or attribute sorcery to members of their own local group and then kill them. Thus scapegoats for the misfortunes are found. Some anthropologists have argued that the identification and killing of real or putative sorcerers is a means by which a local group can rid itself of undesirable members. In their view the killing of sorcerers is beneficial to the local group. It seems more reasonable, however, to interpret the killing of sorcerers as a breakdown in social control. If sorcery promotes social control by deterring individuals from harming each other, it cannot be logically argued that the killing of sorcerers promotes social control. In fact, when a substantial number of individuals "take the law into their own hands" this undermines and threatens the authority and power of the political leaders. If the leader has the power and wishes to assert it, he will intercede and prevent the killing of sorcerers. He may also deem it against the law for unauthorized members of the local group to kill reputed sorcerers. Furthermore, the practice of sorcery itself may be outlawed. If Whiting's analysis is correct, namely that sorcery does not occur in cultures with superordinate control, the above argument provides an explanation for the relationship.

Many anthropologists, both in ethnographies and textbooks, distinguish between sorcery and witchcraft. Just as sorcery requires sorcerers, witchcraft requires witches. But witches, in contrast to sorcerers, are not people who have practiced or employed supernatural means to destroy others. Witches are individuals who have evil intentions and activities attributed to them. Thus the practice of sorcery actually occurs, but the practice of witchcraft is imaginary. Although many anthropologists make this distinction, analysis of actual cultures reveals that this distinction is often difficult to apply. There are some ethnographers who after months of fieldwork are unable to determine whether sorcery is practiced. In these cultures individuals attribute the practice of sorcery to others in the local group, but no one in the local group will ever admit having practiced sorcery. If the ethnographer concludes that witchcraft is present (that is, people believe in sorcery but no one practices it)—but individuals practice sorcery and will not admit it—then he has reached an erroneous conclusion. If he concludes that sorcery is present, his decision is based upon insufficient evidence. Since it is difficult, if not impossible, in some cultures to ascertain whether sorcery is practiced, it seems best not to attempt to distinguish between sorcery and witchcraft.

28. Is sorcery practiced?
    1. no
    2. yes

Sorcery is present if members of the culture deliberately use magic, supernatural beings, or other supernatural powers to attempt to harm or kill others. A problem in classification arises if the ethnographer describes sorcery practices, but states that sorcery is not actually practiced or that he has been unable to find evidence that it is practiced. Although perhaps not a fully satisfactory solution, one way of dealing with the problem is to classify all cultures whose members believe that sorcery is practiced, whether or not there are sorcerers, as being cultures in which sorcery is practiced. In addition, if there is no evidence that sorcery is practiced or there is evidence that it is not practiced, this should be noted.

Sorcery is practiced by Yąnomamö shamans (Chagnon 1968:49):

> The *noreshi* is the vulnerable portion of the complete being, the part that is the target of witchcraft and harmful magic. The shamans (*shabori*) wage constant war against the evil demons (*hekura*) of enemy groups who have been sent to capture the *noreshi* parts of children. They, in turn, send their own *hekura* to capture the *noreshi* of enemy children. . . .
> The vulnerability of the *noreshi* to magical spells is best exemplified by the fact that the shamans of every village spend most of their time chanting to the *hekura* (demons) with the intention of persuading them either to attack the *noreshi* of other (enemy) children or to drive off the *hekura* sent by enemy shamans.

The Qemant believe in and practice sorcery. Magic is used deliberately to harm others (see Question 27 for quotation). One way in which the power to injure others can be obtained is to become a Ganel *sabi* (Gamst 1969:39):

A person may acquire evil powers by entering into a league with Saytan. Such a person is called Ganel *sabi* (Ganel puller). One can also become a Ganel sabi by defecating and urinating at the outer of the three concentric walls of a circular Ethiopian church. As in the tale of Dr. Faustus, the Ganel sabi must pay for his evil powers with his immortal soul. A Ganel sabi can kill people, burn houses from a distance, cure people with Saytan's advice, and cause other fortune or misfortune. The services of a Ganel sabi may be purchased for goods or money.

The Qemant also believe in witches (Gamst 1969:52–53):

It is difficult to find a witch in Qemantland. Few people, Qemant or otherwise, consciously play the role of a witch as they do the roles. of shaman, magician, and diviner. However, the role of a witch is part of the reference group that Qemant and others relate to for guides to behavior; that is, people act and think as though witches do exist. People suspect others of being witches and believe they have felt the effects of witchcraft, even though no one admits to being a witch or perpetrating the associated blight on men, animals, plants, and events.

Gamst's cautious phrasing implies that there may be practitioners of witchcraft. Although the Qemant believe in magicians, Ganel sabi, and witches (conceived as different categories of persons), all three types of practitioners use supernatural means to destroy others; hence, they can be classified as sorcerers.

Post-partum Sex Taboo

The post-partum sex taboo is a rule which prohibits a woman from having sexual intercourse with her husband, or any man, after she has given birth to a child. In the vast majority of cultures such a rule is followed, at least until after the woman's wounds have healed and she has regained her regular menstrual cycle. It was discovered by J. W. M. Whiting, Kluckhohn, and Anthony (1958) in a cross-cultural study of fifty-six cultures that approximately half of the cultures (twenty-seven) had a post-partum sex taboo which lasted for a least a year or more after the woman gave birth. The remaining twenty-nine cultures had a post-partum sex taboo which lasted one year or less. The decision to use one year or twelve months as the dividing line between those cultures with a long and those with a short post-partum sex taboo was based upon the fact that —for some unknown reason—"the duration of the taboo is rarely in the neighborhood of one year" (Stephens 1962:4). Cultures with a long post-partum sex taboo may be divided into two groups. First, there are those cultures located in the disease-ridden tropics whose members often believe that sexual intercourse will sour the mother's milk and whose post-partum sex taboo as a consequence lasts as long as the mother nurses her child, usually two or three years. Second, there are nomadic hunting groups located primarily in North America whose women cannot carry two children on a long march, and as a consequence they deliberately do not have a second child until the first is old enough to walk, which may be as long as four years or more. Thus it appears that a long post-partum sex taboo results in many cultures from a conscious realization that the intentional spacing of children is beneficial for the health of young children and their mothers (J. W. M. Whiting 1959:176–177).

Several factors have been given credit for producing a long post-partum sex taboo. First, general polygyny has been shown to be highly related to the taboo (Stephens 1962:179). In polygynous cultures mothers and children often occupy their own living quarters and husbands occupy separate sleeping quarters or rotate their time between the living quarters of their wives. When a child is born, the separation of spouses which is already built into the domestic system is accentuated. Since the husbands have other wives, a long post-partum sex taboo does not deny them sexual gratification. Thus it is simpler and more likely for a polygynous, rather than a monogamous, culture to adopt a long taboo. Second, clan organization is likewise highly related to the post-partum sex taboo (Young 1965: 118–119). It is argued that the spacing of children is important in cultures where women must work regularly in horticultural activities and must contribute to a group larger than the household. Third, a protein deficiency in the diet, which often occurs in tropical climates, has also been shown to be highly related to the taboo (J. W. M. Whiting 1964). Women in such regions must avoid becoming pregnant in order that their milk will remain rich in protein. Actually, polygyny, clan organization, and protein deficiency are highly related to each other, and probably all three factors are instrumental in producing a long post-partum sex taboo.

Anthropologists originally became interested in the post-partum sex taboo because of its influence upon the Oedipal situation. In psychoanalytic theory the Oedipus complex refers to the sexual attraction of a boy for his mother. This results in feelings of rivalry and hostility towards his father. This has a lasting effect on his personality which may manifest itself in unconscious fantasies, sexual fears and inhibitions, moral standards and guilt, and mental illness. Anthropologists undertaking research on the post-partum sex taboo have argued—although there are slightly different versions of the theory—that a long taboo creates dependency upon the mother, arouses the sexual desire of the male child for his mother, engenders father-son rivalry, and leads to sexual anxiety. And thus cultures with a long post-partum sex taboo will develop beliefs which reflect the psychological conflicts of adult males, and they will develop customs which serve to resolve these conflicts. Several of the beliefs and customs which are supposedly produced by a long post-partum sex taboo are as follows: Adolescent male initiation ceremonies are an institution which breaks the dependency upon the mother and resolves the father-son rivalry (J. W. M. Whiting, Kluckhohn, and Anthony 1958). The importance of sorcery as an explanation for illness, which is a manifestation of paranoia, is a defense against sexual anxiety (J. V. M. Whiting 1959). The elaboration of menstrual taboos is determined by the high level of male castration anxiety which is created by the sexual desire of the child for his mother (Stephens 1962). The avoidance of female in-laws and sisters stems from the fear of sexual contact between the avoiding individuals, the genesis of which lies in the desire for sexual intercourse with the mother (Stephens 1962). Since psychoanalytic theory is not accepted as a valid explanatory system by many anthropologists, it is advisable to only tentatively accept the above theory at the present time.

29. How long is the post-partum sex taboo?
  1. absent
  2. short
  3. long

If there is no rule which prohibits a woman from having sexual intercourse within a month after the birth of a child, the post-partum sex taboo is absent. A month is chosen as the dividing line since it takes nearly a month for a woman's wounds to heal. If there is a rule and it is observed for less than twelve months, the post-partum sex taboo is classified as short. If the post-partum sex taboo is observed for twelve months or more, it is classified as long. Many ethnographies contain detailed information on this topic because the long post-partum sex taboo, although not labeled by this term, has been viewed as one of the unusual customs of primitive cultures. If the exact duration, in months, of the taboo is given, it should be recorded.

For the Yąnomamö the post-partum sex taboo is long. However, the taboo is not always observed. When an unwanted child is born, infanticide is practiced (Chagnon 1968:74,75):

The Yąnomamö have taboos against intercourse when a woman is pregnant or is nursing a child. The taboo is by no means followed to the strict letter, since children are nursed for three years or more—some men sheepishly admit having coitus with a lactating wife. Rerebawä, whose youngest child is about a year old, told me that he recently tried to persuade his wife to make love. He added: "She told me to go take some drugs and chant to my forest spirits; she is still 'stingy' with her vagina."

A child is killed at birth, irrespective of its sex, if the mother already has a nursing baby. They rationalize the practice by asserting that the new infant would probably die anyway, since its older sibling would drink most of the milk. They are most reluctant to jeopardize the health and safety of a nursing child by weaning it before it is three years old or so, preferring to kill the competitor instead.

Although Gamst provides a substantial section on Qemant childbirth (1969:99–102), no information is provided on the post-partum sex taboo. There probably is a short taboo, since it is unlikely that the taboo is absent and since it is likely that the ethnographer would have noted a long taboo (much information on childbirth is given) if it had been present. Nevertheless, one should record that no data are available for answering this question.

Games

Games have always been of interest to anthropologists. Lewis H. Morgan, who along with Edward B. Tylor was one of the two major founders of anthropology, devoted an entire chapter to the discussion of games in his famous ethnography, *League of the Iroquois*, first published in 1851. Many regard this classic work, which describes the customs and way of life of the Iroquois Indians of New York State, as the first ethnography. Morgan discovered that "there were but six principal games among the Iroquois, and these are divisible into athletic games, and games of chance" (1962:291). Athletic games included lacrosse, javelins (spears thrown at rolling hoops), snow snake (a stick thrown across the snow for distance), and archery; games of chance included the game of deer buttons and the peach stone game (both games used lots blackened on one side). Tyler was also interested in games, particularly complex games of strategy such as the nearly identical games of parcheesi (played in India) and patolli (played in Mexico), which could be used to demonstrate that distant cultures had once been in contact (1879).

Not all types of recreational activities or amusements can be considered games. For an activity to be classified as a game it must be "characterized by: (1) organized play, (2) competition, (3) two or more sides, (4) criteria for determining the winner, and (5) agreed-upon rules" (Roberts, Arth, and Bush 1959:597). Games can be classified into the three basic types delineated by such nineteenth-century anthropologists as

Morgan and Tylor: "(1) games of *physical skill*, in which the outcome is determined by the players' motor activities; (2) games of *strategy*, in which the outcome is determined by rational choices among possible courses of action; and (3) games of *chance*, in which the outcome is determined by guesses or by some uncontrolled artifact such as a die or a wheel" (Roberts and Sutton-Smith 1962:166). All three types of games are played by both children and adults.

Games may serve a number of functions in any particular culture. The most obvious function, of course, is recreation. Games, for both participants and onlookers, are usually a pleasant form of entertainment. If betting occurs, valuable goods may be redistributed. Gambling—for winners—can be a profitable way of using one's time. Some anthropologists have viewed games of physical skill as being "safety-valve" mechanisms for releasing pent-up frustrations in harmless ways. Without some controlled means of releasing frustrations, so the argument goes, adult males are likely to engage in warfare, the only available outlet for their hostilities and aggression. If the argument were correct, cultures with games involving physical skill would engage in warfare less frequently than cultures without such games. This relationship does not appear to occur (Sipes n.d.). Rather, there seems to be evidence that many games involving physical skill, such as the Iroquois games of lacrosse, javelins, and archery, provide training in the art of war. Games of physical skill are explicitly recognized by the members of some cultures as providing training for war.

Games are "expressive models"; that is, they are models of various cultural activities and at the same time they serve to express the needs of the players. Since games are models in the sense of being simplified representations of what actually occurs in the world of adults, they are used to teach children (usually indirectly) cultural values, social rules, and techniques for coping with the adult world without subjecting the children to the real consequences of being an adult. But not only do games serve a socialization function, they also provide therapy of sorts for individuals with psychological conflicts. Individiuals with particular types of emotional conflicts are attracted to games—the type they prefer depending upon the nature of their conflict—because games provide a simplified version of the conflict situation. The individual is therefore able to cope with his problems on a reduced scale. Thus the needs of the individual are, at least while the game is being played, satisfied and expressed through the game.

This "expressive models" approach is supported by a series of empirical relationships. Games of physical skill are more likely to be played by peoples living in temperate rather than tropical climates, and those peoples with games of physical skill emphasize rewards for achievement. Presumably individuals who have difficulty in obtaining success in these achievement oriented cultures find relief in participating in games of physical skill. Since games of strategy appear to be models of complex social interactive systems, it is not surprising to find games of strategy in cultures with complex social and political systems. Since the giving and taking of orders is characteristic of these hierarchically organized political communities, it is likewise not surprising to find pressure for obedience present. Presumably individuals who are unsure of their position in the social system but remain obedient to it resolve their ambivalence by winning games of strategy. The sweetest victories are over parents or superiors. Games of chance are found in cultures in which the supernatural beings are benevolent and can be coerced. Reward for responsibility characterizes these cultures. Presumably individuals who perform routine tasks in these responsibility oriented cultures can express feelings of irresponsibility by playing games of chance—such games often involve betting. Both winning and losing may satisfy the emotional conflict (Roberts, Arth, and Bush 1959; Roberts and Sutton-Smith 1962). Although these empirical results support the "expressive models" approach or theory in its general form, the specific theories which purport to explain the relationships between different types of games and different psychological conflict situations are still tentative.

Thus far only the three basic types of games have been discussed. Many games, however, contain elements of two or three of the basic principles: physical skill, strategy, and chance. For example, lacrosse, considered by Morgan to be a game of physical skill, also contains an element of strategy. Logically, in addition to the three basic types, there are three types of games composed of two basic principles and one type of game composed of all three principles. Any of these seven types of games may be played by the members of a culture. It is also possible to discover cultures which do not have games.

30. What types of games are played?
   1. games are absent
   2. physical skill
   3. physical skill and strategy
   4. physical skill and chance
   5. physical skill, strategy, and chance
   6. strategy
   7. strategy and chance
   8. chance

The procedure to be followed in determining what types of games are played is to analyze each game described in the ethnography in terms of the three basic principles. After each game is analyzed it should be recorded by name after one of the seven types. When all games have been analyzed and recorded, not only is it possible to mark (in the left margin) which types are played, but it is also possible to count the number of games per type. Thus a measure of the relative importance of each type of game can be determined. For some cultures a student may wish to list a game which is the only example of its type with several games listed for another type. In cross-cultural studies Roberts and his collaborators often combined games of physical skill and chance with games of physical skill, and games of strategy and chance with games of strategy. They found no examples of games of physical skill, strategy, and chance (Roberts and Sutton-Smith 1962:169).

Games are not described in the Yąnomamö ethnography. Young boys shoot arrows at captured lizards, but this is an amusement, not a game (Chagnon 1968:90–91). An intervillage feast lasting several days is described in detail, but nowhere in the lengthy account of drug taking, dancing, eating, chanting, and dueling are games mentioned or described (Chagnon 1968:105–117).

Chest-pounding duels, side-slapping contests, and club fights do not qualify as games. Although organization, competition, sides, and agreed-upon rules are present, there is no criterion for determining the winner. The side which is taking the worse beating often escalates the fighting to a more violent form of armed combat, such an an axe or machete duel, a spear fight, or a battle with bows and arrows in which men are killed (Chagnon 1968:113–114):

> There were about sixty adult men on each side in the fight, divided into two arenas, each comprised of hosts and guests. Two men, one from each side, would step into the center of the milling, belligerent crowd of weapon-wielding partisans, urged on by their comrades. One would step up, spread his legs apart, bare his chest, and hold his arms behind his back, daring the other to hit him. The opponent would size him up, adjust the man's chest or arms so as to give himself the greatest advantage when he struck, and then step back to deliver his close-fisted blow. The striker would painstakingly adjust his own distance from his victim by measuring his arm length to the man's chest, taking several dry runs before delivering his blow. He would then wind up like a baseball pitcher, but keeping both feet on the ground, and deliver a tremendous wallop with his fist to the man's left pectoral muscle, putting all of his weight into the blow.

Fighters take turns throughout the duel (Chagnon 1968:115):

> At one point Kąobawä's men, sore from the punishment they had taken and worried that they would ultimately lose the fight, wanted to escalate

the contest to an axe duel. Kạobawä was vigorously opposed to this, as he knew it would lead to bloodshed. . . . The fight had still not been decided, although Kạobawä's group seemed to be getting the worst of it. They then insisted on escalating the fighting to side slapping, partly because their chests were too sore to continue in that fashion, and partly because their opponents seemed to have an edge on them.

The side slapping duel is nearly identical in form to chest pounding, except that the blow is delivered with an open hand across the flanks of the opponent, between his rib-cage and pelvis bone. It is a little more severe than chest pounding because casualties are more frequent and tempers grow hotter more rapidly when a group's champion falls to the ground, gasping for wind, and faints.

The duel ended with the guests backing out of the village with arrows drawn in their bows.

Club fights, which result from arguments, may also escalate into brawls in which men are killed (Chagnon 1968:119):

Most duels start between two men, usually after one of them has been caught *en flagrante* trysting with the other's wife. The enraged husband challenges his opponent to strike him on the head with a club. He holds his own club vertically, leans against it and exposes his head for his opponent to strike. After he has sustained a blow on the head, he can then deliver one on the culprit's skull. But as soon as blood starts to flow, almost everybody rips a pole out of the house frame and joins in the fighting, supporting one or the other of the contestants.

For a specific case in which one man died, see Question 20.

Since neither side will admit defeat, there is no criterion for determining the winner. Hence, chest-pounding duels, side-slapping contests, and club fights are not games.

No data on the types of games played are furnished in the Qemant ethnography.

Initiation Rites

Initiation rites are ceremonies, supervised in part by the adults of a culture, which are mandatory for all adolescents of one sex only (Young 1965:12). If the ceremony is mandatory for all boys of a given culture, it is a *male initiation rite*; if it is mandatory for all girls of a given culture, it is a *female initiation rite*. A culture may have both male and female initiation rites. Since initiation rites occur periodically, usually when there are a sufficient number of boys or girls in the local group to be initiated, the adolescents undergoing initiation may range from approximately ten to twenty years of age. Thus for many members of a culture initiation does not occur precisely at puberty. Most anthropologists view initiation rites as ceremonies which mark the passage of an individual from the social status of child to the social status of adult. Thus an initiate goes through a period of social transition in which he gives up one identification for another. Since it is a crisis period for him, the public nature of the ceremony enhances his self-esteem and assists him in assuming a new identification. During the ceremonies the boys or girls are often given instruction in customs which are supposedly known only to adults.

The classic analysis of initiation rites is Arnold van Gennep's treatise on *The Rites of Passage* (1960; orig. 1909). In addition to initiation ceremonies, other rites of passage are those rites related to birth, marriage, and death. For van Gennep a rite of passage was a ceremony of regeneration, a rite of death and rebirth, a transition from the profane to the sacred. He showed that rites of passage can be divided into three consecutive major phases which he called separation, transition, and incorporation. Although recent theories have modified van Gennep's analysis, it nevertheless still provides the basis for all contemporary discussions of initiation ceremonies.

Initiation rites vary in their degree of elaborateness from one culture to another. Young (1965:14–17) has developed a four-step scale of "sex-role dramatization" for measuring the degree of elaborateness of both male and female initiation ceremonies. Each step of the scale represents an increase in dramatization and social participation. The steps are as follows: (1) customary minimal social recognition (gift, party, change of name, and so forth), (2) personal dramatization (initiate is ceremonially dressed or adorned), (3) organized social response (group dresses up and/or performs), and (4) affective social response (beating or severe hazing of initiates). The steps are cumulative. This means, for example, that if male initiation rites in a culture can be classified as "affective social response" (step 4), all three lower items on the scale (steps 1, 2, and 3) are present also. Although Young states that "initiation ceremonies proper begin with step 1" (1965:15), many anthropologists probably would prefer to restrict the definition of initiation rites to include only rites which can be classified as step 3 or step 4, for only those rites involve the active participation of members of the local group. Rites which can be classified as either step 1 or step 2 would not be considered initiation rites since they focus upon individuals and not groups of initiates.

Although initiation rites perform the important function of symbolizing the transition from childhood to adulthood, many cultures do not have any type of initiation ceremonies. In a cross-cultural study of fifty-four cultures Young found that 60 percent of the cultures did not have any male initiation rites and 43 percent did not have any female initiation rites

(1965:15). Moreover, Young found that male initiation rites are more likely than female initiation rites to occur at step 4 on the scale of sex-role dramatization. He thus concludes that "male initiation rites are generally more elaborate or intense than those for females" (1965:16).

Why do some cultures have initiation rites, while others do not? This is a question which anthropologists have been attempting to answer since the time of van Gennep. In the past fifteen years two major explanations have been offered for male initiation rites and two for female rites. J. W. M. Whiting, Kluckhohn, and Anthony (1958) argue that male initiation rites are produced by a long post-partum sex taboo and by a long (over one year) exclusive mother-son sleeping arrangement. These two customs supposedly develop in boys dependence upon their mothers and hostility toward their fathers. According to the theory, male initiation rites break this dependence and resolve the hostility toward the father. Young (1965), who disagrees with Whiting, Kluckhohn, and Anthony, argues that male solidarity—not childhood customs—is responsible for male initiation rites. By male solidarity Young means that there is cooperation in work and war among the men of the local group. The greater the degree of male solidarity, the higher the male initiation rite will rank on the scale of sex-role dramatization. "The dramatization of sex role—initiation rites—is functionally necessary for maintaining the solidarity of men" (1965:41). Anthropologists are undecided as to which theory is correct, if either.

The solidarity theory has also been used by Young (1965) to explain the presence of female initiation rites. He argues that female solidarity is great if there are female work groups and institutionalized household unity present in the culture. The need to maintain female solidarity accounts for female initiation rites. Brown (1963), who has developed a similar theory, argues that in those cultures in which girls continue to reside in the homes of their mothers after marriage (that is, matrilocal residence), the rites represent an announcement of the girls' changed status. This symbolization of adulthood is necessary because the women spend their adult lives in the same households in which they had been children. Brown also shows that female initiation rites are likely to occur in cultures in which women make an important contribution to subsistence activities. These theories have also received only tentative acceptance.

31. What types of initiation rites are present?
   1. initiation rites absent
   2. male initiation rites, step _____
   3. female initiation rites, step _____

As Young has shown, initiation ceremonies, both for boys or for girls, can be ranked on a four-step scale of sex-role dramatization. In addition to determining whether male or female initiation rites are present in the culture, the student should determine at what step of the scale the rites occur. The scale score should be recorded for each type of initiation rite. A zero (0) can be used to indicate an absence of either type of rite.

Among the Yąnomamö, male initiation rites do not occur. On the other hand, female initiation rites, which can be ranked on step two of the scale of sex-role dramatization, do occur (Chagnon 1968:85):

> A girl's transition to womanhood is obvious because of its physiological manifestations. At first menses (*yobömou*) Yąnomamö girls are confined to their houses and hidden behind a screen of leaves. Their old cotton garments are discarded and replaced by new ones manufactured by their mothers or by older female friends. During this week of confinement, the girl is fed by her relatives; her food must be eaten by means of a stick, as she is not allowed to come into contact with it in any other fashion. She must also scratch herself with another set of sticks. . . . After her puberty confinement, a girl is eligible to begin life as a wife and take up residence with her husband.
>
> Males, on the other hand, do not have their transition into manhood marked by a ceremony. Nevertheless, one can usually tell when a boy is attempting to enter the world of men. The most conspicuous sign is his anger when others call him by his name.

Gamst explicitly states that for the Qemant initiation rites are absent (1969:106):

> Marriage (*fahu yewinat*), and the marriage ceremony (*senaw*), constitute a rite of passage from adolescence to young adulthood for Qemant males. This is not always the case for females because of their youth. There is no other coming-of-age ceremony for males or females.

Marriage of course is a rite of passage, but it has not been considered an initiation rite by anthropologists.

Art

Every culture has decorative patterns which may adorn baskets and pottery vessels, tools and weapons, fabrics and clothing, furniture and houses. Sometimes even the human body is decorated—with paint, tattooing, or scarification. In some cultures nonutilitarian objects are produced which can be classified as art objects if they are considered to be beautiful by members of the culture. Both ornamentation and objects of art have been considered to be art. In his 1927 book *Primitive Art*—the classic and probably still most authoritative work on the art of nonliterate peoples—Franz Boas divided the "arts of space" into "graphic arts" and "plastic arts." Graphic or two-dimensional art includes painting, drawing, tattooing, and embroidering; plastic or three-dimensional art includes sculpture and ceramics. Boas classified poetry, music, and dance as "arts of time." Although many of the same principles and conclusions developed in the study of graphic and plastic art apply to the study of poetry, music, and dance, the "arts of time" will not be discussed. The focus of this section will be upon graphic art.

Art may serve a number of different functions both for the artist and for the viewer. First, it affords enjoyment for the artist through "the joy engendered by the mastery of technique and also by the pleasure produced by the perfection of form" (Boas 1955:349). For the viewer it provides enjoyment through an esthetic reaction. Second, art is informative since it permits the artist to express his emotions and thoughts, and it permits the viewer to receive a message. Sometimes an object of art purposely tells a story, as in a wall mural. Third, art is religious. Often the artist produces representations of supernatural beings which may be used in religious ceremonies, and the viewer has a material representation through which he can communicate with the supernatural beings. Fourth, art objects are a sign of status and wealth. Through their production the outstanding artist gains renown, and the viewer, provided he is the owner, has a means of displaying his good taste and his success in the material world. Sometimes art objects are treasures which symbolize the importance of the political community and its leader.

Three types of graphic art can be distinguished. *Abstract* art depends upon formal elements such as lines, triangles, diamonds, squares, circles, with the pattern formed from these elements showing such properties as symmetry, repetition, balance, and rhythm. The pattern is based upon a conscious arrangement of parts. The repetition of motifs produces a simple, and often geometric, pattern. Arbitrary meaning can be assigned to the elements by the artist and other members of his culture if the elements symbolize things in the real or supernatural world, or if natural forms are incorporated into the pattern. Meaning is attached to the individual elements, not the overall pattern. *Representational-expressionistic* art depicts people, animals, or natural phenomena, but the treatment of the figures is exaggerated. The representation is based upon a deliberate over emphasis of certain parts of the figures depicted. Geometric patterns may be used to produce the exaggeration. Since individual, nonrepetitive motifs are employed, the pattern formed is more complex than the pattern in abstract art. In contrast to abstract art, meaning is attached to the overall pattern, not to the individual elements (although certain elements or figures in the design may have meaning). *Representational-naturalistic* art depicts people, animals, or natural phenomena in a realistic manner. The representation is based upon a deliberate attempt to portray things as they appear. Formal elements and geometric patterns are not employed. The pattern formed is in most instances more complex than the pattern in representational-expressionistic art. In naturalistic art, as well as in expressionistic art, meaning is attached to the overall pattern (Hays 1958:147–160).

Nineteenth-century anthropologists were interested in the evolution of art. Some viewed art as evolving from geometric or abstract to naturalistic patterns; others viewed it as evolving from naturalistic to geometric or abstract patterns. Boas (1955) demonstrated the futility of such approaches by showing that abstract and naturalistic art are often found in the same culture. For example, one type of art will be used on certain utilitarian objects, while the other type of art will be employed in the construction of nonutilitarian objects. In some cultures the men produce naturalistic art and the women abstract art. Boas concluded that the types of art, and their particular manifestations, developed by a culture were the outcome of the stimulus of forms in the physical environment, the limitations of the materials used, the motor habits of the artists, the historical contacts which the culture had with other peoples, and the beliefs and values of the members of the culture.

Two cross-cultural studies, both using the same sample of thirty cultures, have shown the relationship of the complexity of design to both child training practices and social stratification. Since expressionistic art is more complex than abstract art and since naturalistic art is more complex than expressionistic art, it is possible to translate the three types of graphic art into a single measure of design complexity which corresponds to the variable or attribute employed in the two cross-cultural studies. This variable "was defined at the upper extreme as a design with many unrepeated figures to form a complex organization of design; the lower extreme of this variable was defined as a design with few figures or repetition of figures to form a simple organization of design" (Barry 1957:380). In the first of these studies, Barry (1957) found that severity of socialization, particularly severe pressures for independence rather than obedience, was characteristic of cultures with complex or naturalistic design patterns. In the other study, Fischer (1961) tested and found support for the theory that cultures with a well-developed social hierarchy will have complex designs, and cultures with an egalitarian social and political system will have simple designs. Underlying his theory is the notion that on a psychological level the elements in a design are "unconscious representations of persons in the society" (1961:81). Since persons are equal in an egalitarian culture, the repetition of the same design elements represents a number of equal comrades; since persons are unequal in a hierarchical culture, they are represented by a variety of distinct elements in the design. These psychological theories, just as the psychological theories described in the three previous sections, have received only tentative acceptance by anthropologists.

32. What types of graphic art are present?
  1. abstract
  2. representational-expressionistic
  3. representational-naturalistic

Since the three types of graphic art vary in design complexity from simple to complex, distinguishing criteria related to complexity should be employed to differentiate the types. Representational art can be distinguished from abstract art by examining the formal elements in the design: if the elements are repeated, it is abstract art; if they are not repeated (that is, the formal elements are different or formal elements are absent), it is representational art. Expressionistic art can be distinguished from naturalistic art by examining the "picture" in the design: if parts of the figures depicted are exaggerated (that is, out of proportion to other parts of the figures), it is expressionistic art; if it appears that the picture is a more or less accurate representation of reality, it is naturalistic art. Since there are conventional ways of handling certain design problems—such as depth perception—in naturalistic art, a picture which does not look like a photograph should not necessarily be classified as expressionistic. For example, American primitive paintings or the paintings of children in the United States should be classified as naturalistic even though they lack perspective. They are naturalistic because the artist attempted to depict reality. If the ethnography contains statements that artists in the culture deliberately distort their figures or that they attempt to accurately depict what they see, more substantial evidence is available for classifying examples according to the two types of representational art.

In classifying types of graphic art, photographs or line drawings in the ethnography may be used. More than one type of graphic art may be present in the culture. All illustrative materials should be examined—including pictures of pottery, weapons, clothing, and houses—for examples of graphic art. In addition to noting the different types of graphic art present, the objects on which the designs occur should be listed. If men produce one type of art, and women another type, this should be recorded. It is worth noting whether three-dimensional art is present.

The Yąnomamö ethnography provides little information on art. Nevertheless, two photographs show circles and wavy lines painted on men's bodies and faces (Chagnon 1968:25,112), Apparently both men and women paint their bodies when intervillage feasts are held (Chagnon 1968:109):

> The men of the host group had finished their preparations for the feast; they were all painted in red and black, bearing colorful feathers. . . .
> While the men were taking their drugs, the women were busy painting and decorating themselves with feathers and red pigment.

In another photograph a woman is wearing a woven belt decorated with diamonds and circles (Chagnon 1968:38). On the basis of these examples, Yąnomamö art can be classified as abstract.

Almost no information on Qemant art is available in the monograph. What little information there is permits one to classify their graphic art as abstract (Gamst 1969:54,105):

> As a neck pendant, the case [of the amulet] is regarded as decorative. The parchment is inscribed in Geez or Arabic with mixed characters or with phrases from the Bible or Koran. Figures and geometric designs may be included.

> Tattooing is a common form of adornment and is done on the upper gums, neck, chest, forehead, hand, lower forearm, and ankles. Nug oil and soot are heated together to make a dark blue dye for the tattoos, which are done by puncturing the skin repeatedly with the thorns of a variety of acacia tree dipped into the pigment. In addition to being decorative, tattoos serve therapeutic and protective functions.

CHAPTER **6**

Conclusion

The sections of this volume have dealt with thirty-two topics. Each section has described one or more of the important concepts used by anthropologists, concepts which make up the basic vocabulary of cultural anthropology. They are used as guidelines in collecting data in a field situation and in gleaning information from published accounts. If the concepts are used to summarize the way of life of a culture, they become the vehicle by which an ethnographer communicates with his reader—the concepts represent the reality which was observed. They are also used by anthropologists in comparative research. Any attempt to compare two or more cultures in terms of their similarities or differences will employ these important concepts, as will any discussion which purports to explain why certain beliefs and practices occur. For example: Why are the Yạnomamö polygynous? Why are some peoples polygynous and not others? Why are a majority of the world's cultures polygynous? Anthropologists cannot have a discussion—orally or in print—without using many of the concepts defined in the previous chapters.

Within each section a question was stated. The answers to the questions were concepts. Each question asked: For the particular culture which I am now studying, which concepts represent culture traits present? The answers of course also provided information on which concepts were not represented by culture traits. The thirty-two topics are listed on the following table, and the questions are listed exactly as they appear in the text on data sheets at the end of this chapter. At the end of each section there was a discussion and usually a quotation from Chagnon's ethnographic account of the Yạnomamö (1968) and from Gamst's study of the Qemant (1969). These discussions provided information on culture traits which were present in Yạnomamö culture and in Qemant culture. This information is summarized on the following table—after each topic is listed the concept which represents the culture trait which is characteristic of either the Yạnomamö or the Qemant. A perusal of the first column of the table provides a "thumbnail" or brief ethnographic sketch of Yạnomamö culture; the second column, an ethnographic sketch of Qemant culture. The sketches are presented almost entirely in terms of anthropological concepts.

Table 2. Summary Analysis of Cultures

Topics	Cultures	
	Yąnomamö	Qemant
1. physical environment	tropical forest, mountains	mountains, desert, grassland, temperate forest
2. subsistence technology	horticulture	agriculture
3. population density	.25 persons per square mile	15 persons per square mile
4. subsistence participation	males predominate	males predominate
5. division of labor	part-time specialists	part-time and full-time specialists
6. settlement pattern	compact villages	dispersed homesteads
7. settlement size	250 persons	2640 persons
8. local economy	balanced reciprocity between households	market exchange
9. economy of culture	balanced reciprocity between local groups	market exchange

10. residence	commonlocal, virilocal	patrilocal, matrilocal, commonlocal, virilocal
11. marriage	general polygyny	monogamy
12. household type	independent nuclear and polygamous family households	independent nuclear and extended family households
13. descent groups	patrilineages	patrilineages, clans, moieties
14. kindreds	absent	kindreds, as quasi-groups
15. cousin marriage	matrilateral and patrilateral cross-cousin marriage	first cousin marriage absent
16. kinship terminology	Iroquois	Eskimo
17. political communities	homogeneous, 125 political communities	heterogeneous, 70 cultures
18. political system	one level	5 levels
19. political leaders	headmen	king, chiefs, headmen
20. legal system	law absent	law of public delicts, law of private delicts

Table 2—Continued

Topics	Cultures	
	Yąnomamö	Qemant
21. military organizations	composed of non-professional warriors	composed of professional warriors
22. feuding	feuding without compensation	feuding absent
23. warfare	continually	not applicable
24. causes of war	revenge, defense, and plunder	defense, revenge, land, subjugation and tribute
25. supernatural beings	superior gods, nonhuman spirits	a high god, superior gods, ancestral and nonhuman spirits
26. religious practitioners	shamans	shamans and priests
27. magic	homeopathic magic	magic present—unclassifiable
28. sorcery	sorcery present	sorcery present
29. post-partum sex taboo	long	no data
30. games	games are absent	no data
31. initiation rites	female initiation rites, step 2	initiation rites absent
32. art	abstract	abstract

The Comparison of Cultures and Culture Traits

The table titled "Summary Analysis of Cultures" on pp. 128–130 can be used to compare cultures and culture traits. Space for 3 blank columns is provided on the table. After a culture has been analyzed and the information recorded on a data sheet containing the thirty-two questions, the culture traits present in that culture can be listed in one of the blank columns; that is, the concepts which represent the culture traits. Culture traits from other cultures can be listed in the remaining columns. (If more than 3 cultures are analyzed, a new table can be made on which to list the culture traits present in each culture.)

When information on two or more cultures has been gathered using a set of questions such as those on the data sheet, the cultures can be compared and contrasted. The use of the same questions permits systematic comparison of the cultures. The table is useful in conducting such a comparison—it is a simple matter to count the number of culture traits which are the same and the number which are different. Generally speaking, the greater the number of culture traits which are the same, the more similar are the cultures. And conversely, the greater the number of culture traits which are different, the less alike are the cultures. For example, the Yąnomamö and the Qemant are highly dissimilar; inspection of the table reveals that twenty-seven out of thirty topics differ, for which there are data for both cultures. Moreover, this method of comparison can be applied to the study of a single culture if two different ethnographic accounts —done at two points in time—are available. It is thus possible to compare the culture at two time periods in the same manner that one would compare two cultures. Any differences can be attributed to changes which have occurred in the culture since it was first studied.

The following example focuses on changes in household types within the same culture at two points in time. In order to keep the example simple, changes in other culture traits are not considered. In 1959 and 1961 I conducted an ethnographic study of several small Negro villages in the Bahama Islands. Using census forms, I collected data from every household in four villages. From the census reports I was able to compute the frequency of household types. In 1961, 38 percent of the households were independent nuclear family households and 18 percent were extended family households. Of the remaining households, 29 percent were headed by single females and 15 percent were headed by single males. In 1968 I returned to the villages and again took a census of every household. Computation of the frequency of household types revealed that the percentages had changed. Thirty percent of the households were independent nuclear family households, a decline of 8 percent, and 27 percent were extended family households, an increase of 9 percent. Of the remaining households, 30 percent were headed by single females and 13 percent were headed by single males (Otterbein 1970b). If the trend has continued, the dominant household type has changed from independent nuclear family households to extended family households.

If one question from the data sheet is used to collect information from a substantial number of cultures, perhaps thirty or more, it is possible to compute the frequency with which different culture traits occur. The cultures may be from a restricted geographical region such as the American South West, from a continental area such as North America, or they may be chosen to represent all parts of the world. Computation of frequencies, in percentages, makes it possible for the anthropologist to reach a conclusion regarding the rarity or prevalence of certain culture traits, either on a regional or worldwide basis. A number of examples are provided in the text: A study of 554 cultures showed that 24 percent of the world's cultures were monogamous, 75 percent were polygynous, and 1 percent were polyandrous. This study demonstrated the rarity of polyandry and the common occurrence of polygyny. A much smaller study of thirty-three cultures which practice either matrilateral or patrilateral cross-cousin marriage revealed that only seven cultures (21 percent) practice patrilateral cross-cousin marriage. Thus it was demonstrated that this form of cross-cousin marriage is more rare than the matrilateral form. Another study, this time of fifty cultures, provided evidence that most cultures have military organizations by showing that only four cultures (8 percent) did not have military organizations. A study of supernatural beings found that nineteen (49 percent) out of thirty-nine cultures had a belief in a high god, twenty-nine (55 percent) out of forty-nine cultures had a belief in one or more superior gods, and thirty-three (67 percent) out of forty-nine cultures had a belief in active ancestral spirits. Thus it is to be expected that many cultures will have more than one type of supernatural being. The long post-partum sex taboo—a custom which one might think would be rare—was found present in twenty-seven (49 percent) out of fifty-six cultures. And in a study of initiation rites in fifty-four cultures it was shown that 40 percent of the cultures had male initiation rites and 57 percent had female initiation rites. Thus initiation rites for both sexes commonly occur.

Given a substantial number of cultures, it is also possible for an anthropologist to locate geographically cultures which are characterized by a particular culture trait. The cultures can be from a region, from a continent, or from the world as a whole. Once the cultures are plotted on a map, it is readily apparent if these culture traits cluster geographically. That is, some culture traits, rather than being evenly distributed over the earth's surface, may be concentrated in specific geographic regions. This concentration may be due to the influence of the physical environment, or a process known as diffusion may be operating. *Diffusion* is the geographic spread of culture traits; it can occur through the acceptance of culture traits from one culture by the members of another culture, or it can occur through the migration or dispersion of local groups belonging to one culture. Only one example of locating geographically those cultures which have a particular trait is given in the text. A long post-partum sex taboo is found primarily in the disease-ridden tropics and in regions of North America inhabited by nomadic hunting groups. This geographical distribution led J. W. M. Whiting (1959) to conclude that a long post-partum sex taboo results from a conscious realization that the intentional spacing of children is beneficial for the health of young children. The physical environment is chiefly responsible for the poor health of children that necessitates their spacing.

Linkages and Hypotheses

Ethnographies, in addition to being descriptions of the cultures of particular groups of people, are also descriptions of how particular cultures are integrated. The basic technique employed by ethnographers to demonstrate the integration of cultures consists of describing *linkages* between culture traits. An example of such a linkage would be the statement that the members of such-and-such culture have a nomadic settlement pattern because their hunting and gathering mode of subsistence prevents the formation of year-round settlements. Thus a linkage connects two culture traits. If the culture traits are designated as *a* and *b*, the linkage can be diagramed as follows:

Culture traits can be linked in more complex ways. For example, three traits can be connected, producing three linkages. This can be diagramed as follows:

Four interconnected culture traits, as shown in the following diagram, produce six linkages:

Each culture trait is shown related to each of the other culture traits. On the other hand, several culture traits can be connected to a single culture trait while not being linked to each other, as the following diagram shows:

Although an ethnographer may have "seen" certain linkages and combinations of linkages while he was conducting fieldwork, it is not until he analyzes his field data that these linkages become crystallized in his mind. That is, they become apparent to him at that stage in the analysis when he is reading and rereading his information and is organizing and reorganizing his topical outline. Once the linkages have been formulated, the ethnographer can proceed with the writing of the report. These linkages become the focal points around which the ethnography is written. Thus an ethnography is not only a description of the culture of a particular group of people, but also a description of how the culture is integrated.

Linkages are of three different types. It should be clear from the above discussion of the procedure followed by an ethnographer in delineating linkages that they are inferences made by the ethnographer. They are not ethnographic data. Since they are inferences, they must be examined for their validity. The first type of linkage—and it is the only type of valid linkage—is the functional relationship. In a functional relationship two culture traits are linked such that they are both mutually dependent; that is, a change in one trait produces a change in the other. Mathematicians show this relationship as follows: $x = y$ (x is a function of y, and y is a function of x; that is, a change in x produces a change in y, and vice versa). When a functional relationship is found to exist, it can be stated that the linkage is a valid one. In other words, a true or real relationship is being described by the linkage. The second type of linkage—and it is not a valid linkage—is the nonfunctional or concomitant relationship. The two traits are found together, but a change in one does not produce a change in the other, since they are not mutually dependent. In fact, it is more precise not to speak of this type of linkage as being a relationship, since it is a linkage based upon a inferred, but invalid, relationship. The ethnographer has put together two or more culture traits which are not functionally related. The third type of linkage is the tautological relationship. A relationship exists between the two traits, or rather the concepts representing the traits, but it results from overlapping definitions. For example, there is a relationship between monogamy and independent nuclear family households. By definition, an independent nuclear family household is a domestic group consisting of a married couple (that is, one man married to one woman) and their children; monogamy, by definition, is the marriage of one man to one woman. Thus the presence of monogamy is one part of the definition of an independent nuclear family household. Therefore, overlapping definitions create a logical relationship. In the language of logic the linkage is said to be tautological.

Linkages of either the functional or nonfunctional type are hypotheses. The only difference between linkages and hypotheses is that linkages usually purport to be valid, true, or real relationships, while hypotheses are usually considered to be statements of relationships which need to be tested to determine their validity. Linkages and hypotheses are thus the same in terms of their basic structure. Although tautological linkages can be considered hypotheses, they should not be so treated, since the relationships between their concepts are derived only from overlapping definitions. As was indicated in the preceding paragraph, some linkages are valid and others are invalid. A hypothesis is a linkage which an anthropologist wishes to test; that is, he wishes to determine the validity of the linkage. If the relationship described by the linkage is precisely stated in the ethnography, it is an explicit hypothesis and is ready for testing. If the relationship is only implied or vaguely described, the linkage is an implicit hypothesis, and should be rephrased in a more explicit fashion before testing; that is, it should be converted into an explicit hypothesis. This process of converting vaguely described linkages into explicit hypotheses is known as deriving hypotheses. It is only through the testing of a hypothesis and the determination of its validity that one can establish whether the linkage described is functional or nonfunctional. If a hypothesis is tested and found to be valid, then the linkage from which it was derived is a description of a functional relationship. If the hypothesis is tested and found to be invalid, then the linkage from which it was derived is a description of a nonfunctional or concomitant relationship. Thus the classification of linkages by type can only be accomplished if the linkages are treated as hypotheses and subjected to testing.

The Testing of Hypotheses

A *hypothesis* is a statement of a precise relationship between that which is to be explained and that which is to do the explaining—a relationship between two variables. When an anthropologist attempts to explain why a certain culture trait occurs, he formulates a hypothesis. Hypotheses usually take one of the following forms: (1) An invariable relationship: if A, then B. (2) A direct relationship: the greater (or higher, or larger) A, the greater (or higher, or larger) B. (3) An inverse relationship: the greater (or higher, or larger) A, the less (or lower, or smaller) B.

In order to test a hypothesis, the variables stated in the hypothesis must be indexed. To index a variable is to establish a series of values for the variable. Variables may have two or more values, and each value must be defined. In deriving a hypothesis some of the thirty-two questions on the data sheet may be used directly as variables. They are the questions for which there is only one "answer." (Questions for which there can be several "answers" can be used as variables if they are separated into more than one question, each question having a single "answer.") The "answers" or concepts which accompany these questions correspond to values, and the definition of each concept corresponds to the definition of each value. Sometimes the values or concepts are referred to as points or categories on the variable. Hypotheses which state the conditions under which certain things will occur—invariable relationships—usually employ two-valued variables, while hypotheses which state either direct or inverse relationships often employ variables which have more than two values. Thus the type of variables used will depend to a great extent upon the manner in which the hypotheses have been formulated.

If an anthropologist is interested only in whether a particular culture trait is to be found or not found in a culture, he employs a two-valued or dichotomous variable. The presence or absence of the culture trait—or rather the concept which represents it—constitutes such a variable, since "present" is one value and "absent" is the other value. A definition of the concept is attached to the "present" value, and the definition of the "absent" value is simply the statement that the phenomenon is not found in the culture. The presence or absence of sorcery (Question 28) is an example of a dichotomous variable. Other questions on the data sheet can be converted into dichotomous variables by placing any concept that appears on the data sheet in a question which has the following form:

Is (or are) _____ practiced (or present)?
1. no
2. yes

Many of the questions on the data sheet may be used as multivalued variables. They are questions for which three or more possible, mutually exclusive "answers" are listed or, in the case of computed numerical answers, can be derived. The classification of the occurrence of internal warfare as continual, frequent, infrequent, or never (Question 23) is an example of a multivalued variable. Many of these more complicated variables require a definition for each of the values of the variable. However, some variables—such as population size of largest settlement (Question 7) or number of hierarchical levels in the political system (Question 18)—do not require a definition for each possible value. Other variables which make use of a formula—such as population density (Question 3)—require a definition for each component of the formula.

The basic way in which a hypothesis is tested is to examine a culture for the purpose of determining whether the culture conforms to the hypothesis. If both the culture trait which is to be explained and the culture trait which is presumed responsible for that culture trait are present in the culture, the hypothesis is confirmed. If either culture trait is absent, the hypothesis is disconfirmed. If both culture traits are absent, the hypothesis is neither confirmed nor disconfirmed. The logic of hypothesis testing is set forth in the following paradigm. A and B represent two culture traits in a hypothesis which has the form: if A, then B.

Hypothesis:	If (A) ,	then (B) .
Confirmed	A present	B present
Disconfirmed	A present	B absent
Disconfirmed	A absent	B present
Neither confirmed nor disconfirmed	A absent	B absent

(The same basic logic applies to statements which hypothesize either a direct or indirect relationship.)

Although the presence of both culture traits in a particular culture confirms the hypothesis, this confirmation is only tentative. When an anthropologist examines one culture, or one culture at a time, he cannot be certain that some unconsidered variable other than the variable given in the hypothesis may better explain the culture trait. In order to demonstrate that other factors (such as the physical environment) or culture traits are not influencing the culture trait which he wishes to explain, it is necessary for the anthropologist to "control" these factors by special techniques. One technique is known as the method of *controlled comparison*. This technique requires that the anthropologist examine two similar cultures simultaneously. The cultures are compared in terms of a series of culture traits. The cultures must be so similar that all the culture traits compared must be the same except for the two culture traits which are stated in the hypothesis. These two culture traits must be present in one of the cultures and absent in the other. Although it is often difficult to find two cultures which meet these requirements, the finding of two such cultures not only confirms the hypothesis, but also rules out as influencing factors those culture traits which are the same in both cultures. (Since local groups within the same culture often differ slightly from each other, such groups can sometimes be used in controlled comparisons.) This technique still does not control or rule out culture traits which are not compared. The thirty-two topics discussed in this book provide an excellent list of culture traits which can be used in controlled comparisons.

The following example of a controlled comparison tests the hypothesis that ambilineages and ambilineal descent are the result of a scarcity of land. The argument underlying this hypothesis is that in cultures where land is plentiful and controlled by unrestricted descent groups based on multi-lineal descent, an increase in population will lead to a shortage of land, which in turn will result in some of the members being excluded from the unrestricted descent groups. Those excluded will be those members not living on the land. Once certain lines of descent are excluded from the unrestricted descent groups, they become converted into ambilineages. Thus an increase in population density will result in the formation of ambi-lineages. For the hypothesis to be confirmed a culture must be found in which the population density is high and ambilineages are present. Jamaica is such a culture. The population density of Jamaica is 230 persons per square mile, and Jamaica has ambilineages. To control for factors other than population density, a culture similar to Jamaica must be found, but it must have a low population density and unrestricted descent groups must be present. A culture meeting these requirements is the Bahamas. The population density of the Bahamas is 15 persons per square mile, and the Bahamas has unrestricted descent groups. In the actual controlled compari-son which was conducted, thirteen culture traits, excluding the two stated in the hypothesis, were compared. The culture traits controlled included kindreds, ambilocal residence, ancestor worship, and a number of factors specific only to the two cultures and the British West Indies. Thus the hypothesis is confirmed, and thirteen culture traits have been ruled out as possible explanatory factors (Otterbein 1964).

Another technique for testing hypotheses is the *cross-cultural survey*. This technique requires that the anthropologist examine a large number of cultures simultaneously. The cultures should be chosen to represent all parts of the world, and they all should be chosen before any of the data is collected. The cultures are analyzed in terms of the two concepts which are stated in the hypothesis. For analyzing the cultures a table, known as a 2×2 contingency table, is constructed. The following table, which has four empty cells designated by Roman numerals, is based upon the paradigm presented to illustrate the logic of hypothesis testing. As in the paradigm, A and B represent two culture traits in a hypothesis which has the form: if A, then B.

	B absent	B present
A present	I	II
A absent	III	IV

After the data on both culture traits have been collected for each culture in the study, cultures which have A present and B absent should be placed in cell I, cultures which have A present and B present should be placed in cell II, cultures which have A absent and B absent should be placed in cell III, and cultures which have A absent and B present should be placed in cell IV. The names of the cultures should actually be recorded in the appropriate cells of the table. It is the cultures in cell II which confirm the hypothesis (cultures in cell III serve to support the hypothesis by not disconfirming it). The cultures in cells I and IV disconfirm the hypothesis. Thus if the majority of cultures in the study are placed in cells II and III, the hypothesis is tentatively confirmed. However, if the majority of cultures are in cells I and IV, the hypothesis is disconfirmed. The number of cultures in each cell can be counted, and percentages can be computed. There are statistical tests which measure the degree of association between the two variables and which determine whether chance could have produced the distribution of cultures in the cells. Any introductory statistics textbook will provide the procedures and formulae to be used. A more technical discussion of the procedure is given in my article titled "Basic Steps in Conducting a Cross-Cultural Study" (Otterbein 1969).

The results of a number of cross-cultural studies have been discussed in the text. In one study reviewed (Otterbein and Otterbein 1965: 1473) the following hypothesis was tested: patrilocal residence produces feuding. (The explanation for this relationship is described in the section dealing with feuding.) Fifty cultures, twenty-five with patrilocal residence and twenty-five with other types of residence, were examined for the presence of feuding. Twenty-two of the cultures had either feuding with compensation or feuding without compensation. The frequencies are shown in the following table.

	Feuding absent	Feuding present
Patrilocal residence present	10	15
Patrilocal residence absent	18	7

Thirty-three of the cultures confirm the hypothesis; seventeen disconfirm the hypothesis. Thus the hypothesis was tentatively confirmed. Appropriate statistical tests added further support (Otterbein and Otterbein 1965:1473).

This book has laid out in systematic fashion the conceptual order of anthropology. Many of the important topics and most of the basic concepts of cultural anthropology have been set forth in the preceding chapters.

Mastery of this conceptual order is a prerequisite to obtaining competence as a professional anthropologist. Whether or not he has the time or desire to become a professional anthropologist and undertake fieldwork, the beginning student of anthropology can—with the aid of the questions and concepts in this book—simulate the methods of the ethnographer by analyzing the detailed descriptions of various customs or culture traits which are contained within ethnographies. For this book presents a way of learning about a culture that is like that of the anthropologist's as he studies a people, then organizes the data, and writes his ethnography. Thus the book has provided a framework for students to use in studying the way of life of a particular people, as that way of life is described by an anthropologist in an ethnography. This conceptual framework permeates every stage of the anthropological enterprise, from fieldwork to writing the ethnography to conducting comparative research.

Data Sheet

Name of Culture _____ Ethnographer_____

Title of Ethnography _____

1. In what type of physical environment is the culture located?
   1. desert
   2. tropical forest
   3. Mediterranean scrub forest
   4. temperate forest
   5. grassland
   6. boreal forest
   7. polar land
   8. mountains

2. What subsistence technology is dominant (or codominant)?
   1. hunting and gathering
   2. animal husbandry
   3. horticulture
   4. agriculture

3. What is the population density of the culture? _____

4. Who plays the major role in the dominant (or codominant) subsistence technology?
   1. males predominate
   2. females predominate
   3. equal participation by both sexes
   4. specialists

5. What is the division of labor?
   1. age and sex only
   2. part-time specialists
   3. full-time specialists

6. What is the settlement pattern?
   1. nomadic
   2. seminomadic
   3. dispersed homesteads
   4. hamlets and/or compact villages
   5. towns and/or cities

7. What is the population of the largest settlement? _____

8. Which principle of exchange is dominant in the local group?
   1. balanced reciprocity between households
   2. generalized reciprocity between households
   3. redistribution through a local allocative agency
   4. market exchange

9. Which principle of exchange is integrative for the entire culture?
   1. none; that is, no patterned exchange between local groups
   2. balanced reciprocity between local groups
   3. generalized reciprocity between local groups
   4. redistribution through a nonlocal allocative center
   5. market exchange

10. What type of marital residence is practiced?
    1. ambilocal
    2. patrilocal
    3. matrilocal
    4. avunculocal
    5. neolocal
    6. virilocal
    7. uxorilocal
    8. commonlocal

11. What type of marriage is practiced?
    1. monogamy
    2. limited polygyny
    3. general polygyny
    4. polyandry

12. What types of households are present?
    1. independent nuclear family
    2. independent polygamous family
    3. extended family
    4. stem family

13. What types of descent groups are present?
    1. descent groups absent
    2. patrilineages
    3. matrilineages
    4. ambilineages
    5. unrestricted descent groups
    6. clans
    7. phratries
    8. moieties

14. What types of kindreds are present?
    1. kindreds absent
    2. kindreds, as categories of kin
    3. kindreds, as quasigroups

15. What types of first cousin marriage are practiced?
    1. first cousin marriage absent
    2. matrilateral cross-cousin marriage
    3. patrilateral cross-cousin marriage
    4. parallel cousin marriage

16. What type of kinship terminology for first cousins is employed?
    1. Hawaiian
    2. Eskimo
    3. Sudanese
    4. Iroquois
    5. Crow
    6. Omaha

17. Are the political communities culturally homogeneous or heterogeneous?
    1. If homogeneous, how many political communities are there in the culture? _____
    2. If heterogeneous, how many cultures are included in the political community? _____

18. How many hierarchical levels are there in the political system? _____

19. What type of political leader is present?
    1. king
    2. dictator
    3. chief
    4. headman

20. What types of law are present?
    1. law absent
    2. law of private delicts (based upon restitutive sanctions)
    3. law of public delicts (based upon penal sanctions)

21. What type of military organization is present?
    1. a military organization is absent
    2. a military organization composed of professional warriors
    3. a military organization composed of both professional and nonprofessional warriors
    4. a military organization composed of nonprofessional warriors

22. Is feuding present?
    1. absent
    2. feuding with compensation
    3. feuding without compensation

23. If there is more than one political community within the culture, how frequently do they war with each other?
    1. continually
    2. frequently
    3. infrequently
    4. never

24. For what reasons does the military organization go to war?
    1. subjugation and tribute
    2. land
    3. plunder
    4. trophies and honors
    5. revenge
    6. defense

25. In what types of supernatural beings do the people believe?
    1. a high god
    2. superior gods
    3. ancestral spirits
    4. nonhuman spirits

26. What types of religious practitioners are present?
    1. absent
    2. shamans
    3. priests

27. What types of magic are practiced?
    1. homeopathic magic
    2. contagious magic

28. Is sorcery practiced?
    1. no
    2. yes

29. How long is the post-partum sex taboo?
    1. absent
    2. short
    3. long

30. What types of games are played?
    1. games absent
    2. physical skill
    3. physical skill and strategy
    4. physical skill and chance
    5. physical skill, strategy, and chance
    6. strategy
    7. strategy and chance
    8. chance

31. What types of initiation rites are present?
    1. initiation rites absent
    2. male initiation rites, step ————
    3. female initiation rites, step ————

32. What types of graphic art are present?
    1. abstract
    2. representational–expressionistic
    3. representational–naturalistic

Data Sheet

Name of Culture _____ Ethnographer_____

Title of Ethnography _____

1. In what type of physical environment is the culture located?
    1. desert
    2. tropical forest
    3. Mediterranean scrub forest
    4. temperate forest
    5. grassland
    6. boreal forest
    7. polar land
    8. mountains

2. What subsistence technology is dominant (or codominant)?
    1. hunting and gathering
    2. animal husbandry
    3. horticulture
    4. agriculture

3. What is the population density of the culture? _____

4. Who plays the major role in the dominant (or codominant) subsistence technology?
    1. males predominate
    2. females predominate
    3. equal participation by both sexes
    4. specialists

5. What is the division of labor?
    1. age and sex only
    2. part-time specialists
    3. full-time specialists

6. What is the settlement pattern?
    1. nomadic
    2. seminomadic
    3. dispersed homesteads
    4. hamlets and/or compact villages
    5. towns and/or cities

7. What is the population of the largest settlement? _____

8. Which principle of exchange is dominant in the local group?
   1. balanced reciprocity between households
   2. generalized reciprocity between households
   3. redistribution through a local allocative agency
   4. market exchange

9. Which principle of exchange is integrative for the entire culture?
   1. none; that is, no patterned exchange between local groups
   2. balanced reciprocity between local groups
   3. generalized reciprocity between local groups
   4. redistribution through a nonlocal allocative center
   5. market exchange

10. What type of marital residence is practiced?
    1. ambilocal
    2. patrilocal
    3. matrilocal
    4. avunculocal
    5. neolocal
    6. virilocal
    7. uxorilocal
    8. commonlocal

11. What type of marriage is practiced?
    1. monogamy
    2. limited polygyny
    3. general polygyny
    4. polyandry

12. What types of households are present?
    1. independent nuclear family
    2. independent polygamous family
    3. extended family
    4. stem family

13. What types of descent groups are present?
    1. descent groups absent
    2. patrilineages
    3. matrilineages
    4. ambilineages
    5. unrestricted descent groups
    6. clans
    7. phratries
    8. moieties

14. What types of kindreds are present?
    1. kindreds absent
    2. kindreds, as categories of kin
    3. kindreds, as quasigroups

15. What types of first cousin marriage are practiced?
    1. first cousin marriage absent
    2. matrilateral cross-cousin marriage
    3. patrilateral cross-cousin marriage
    4. parallel cousin marriage

16. What type of kinship terminology for first cousins is employed?
    1. Hawaiian
    2. Eskimo
    3. Sudanese
    4. Iroquois
    5. Crow
    6. Omaha

17. Are the political communities culturally homogeneous or heterogeneous?
    1. If homogeneous, how many political communities are there in the culture? _____
    2. If heterogeneous, how many cultures are included in the political community? _____

18. How many hierarchical levels are there in the political system? _____

19. What type of political leader is present?
    1. king
    2. dictator
    3. chief
    4. headman

20. What types of law are present?
    1. law absent
    2. law of private delicts (based upon restitutive sanctions)
    3. law of public delicts (based upon penal sanctions)

21. What type of military organization is present?
    1. a military organization is absent
    2. a military organization composed of professional warriors
    3. a military organization composed of both professional and nonprofessional warriors
    4. a military organization composed of nonprofessional warriors

22. Is feuding present?
    1. absent
    2. feuding with compensation
    3. feuding without compensation

23. If there is more than one political community within the culture, how frequently do they war with each other?
    1. continually
    2. frequently
    3. infrequently
    4. never

24. For what reasons does the military organization go to war?
    1. subjugation and tribute
    2. land
    3. plunder
    4. trophies and honors
    5. revenge
    6. defense

25. In what types of supernatural beings do the people believe?
    1. a high god
    2. superior gods
    3. ancestral spirits
    4. nonhuman spirits

26. What types of religious practitioners are present?
    1. absent
    2. shamans
    3. priests

27. What types of magic are practiced?
    1. homeopathic magic
    2. contagious magic

28. Is sorcery practiced?
    1. no
    2. yes

29. How long is the post-partum sex taboo?
    1. absent
    2. short
    3. long

30. What types of games are played?
    1. games absent
    2. physical skill
    3. physical skill and strategy
    4. physical skill and chance
    5. physical skill, strategy, and chance
    6. strategy
    7. strategy and chance
    8. chance

31. What types of initiation rites are present?
    1. initiation rites absent
    2. male initiation rites, step ————
    3. female initiation rites, step ————

32. What types of graphic art are present?
    1. abstract
    2. representational–expressionistic
    3. representational–naturalistic

Data Sheet

Name of Culture _____ Ethnographer_____

Title of Ethnography _____

1. In what type of physical environment is the culture located?
   1. desert
   2. tropical forest
   3. Mediterranean scrub forest
   4. temperate forest
   5. grassland
   6. boreal forest
   7. polar land
   8. mountains

2. What subsistence technology is dominant (or codominant)?
   1. hunting and gathering
   2. animal husbandry
   3. horticulture
   4. agriculture

3. What is the population density of the culture? _____

4. Who plays the major role in the dominant (or codominant) subsistence technology?
   1. males predominate
   2. females predominate
   3. equal participation by both sexes
   4. specialists

5. What is the division of labor?
   1. age and sex only
   2. part-time specialists
   3. full-time specialists

6. What is the settlement pattern?
   1. nomadic
   2. seminomadic
   3. dispersed homesteads
   4. hamlets and/or compact villages
   5. towns and/or cities

7. What is the population of the largest settlement? _____

151

8. Which principle of exchange is dominant in the local group?
   1. balanced reciprocity between households
   2. generalized reciprocity between households
   3. redistribution through a local allocative agency
   4. market exchange

9. Which principle of exchange is integrative for the entire culture?
   1. none; that is, no patterned exchange between local groups
   2. balanced reciprocity between local groups
   3. generalized reciprocity between local groups
   4. redistribution through a nonlocal allocative center
   5. market exchange

10. What type of marital residence is practiced?
    1. ambilocal
    2. patrilocal
    3. matrilocal
    4. avunculocal
    5. neolocal
    6. virilocal
    7. uxorilocal
    8. commonlocal

11. What type of marriage is practiced?
    1. monogamy
    2. limited polygyny
    3. general polygyny
    4. polyandry

12. What types of households are present?
    1. independent nuclear family
    2. independent polygamous family
    3. extended family
    4. stem family

13. What types of descent groups are present?
    1. descent groups absent
    2. patrilineages
    3. matrilineages
    4. ambilineages
    5. unrestricted descent groups
    6. clans
    7. phratries
    8. moieties

14. What types of kindreds are present?
    1. kindreds absent
    2. kindreds, as categories of kin
    3. kindreds, as quasigroups

15. What types of first cousin marriage are practiced?
    1. first cousin marriage absent
    2. matrilateral cross-cousin marriage
    3. patrilateral cross-cousin marriage
    4. parallel cousin marriage

16. What type of kinship terminology for first cousins is employed?
    1. Hawaiian
    2. Eskimo
    3. Sudanese
    4. Iroquois
    5. Crow
    6. Omaha

17. Are the political communities culturally homogeneous or heterogeneous?
    1. If homogeneous, how many political communities are there in the culture? _____
    2. If heterogeneous, how many cultures are included in the political community? _____

18. How many hierarchical levels are there in the political system? _____

19. What type of political leader is present?
    1. king
    2. dictator
    3. chief
    4. headman

20. What types of law are present?
    1. law absent
    2. law of private delicts (based upon restitutive sanctions)
    3. law of public delicts (based upon penal sanctions)

21. What type of military organization is present?
    1. a military organization is absent
    2. a military organization composed of professional warriors
    3. a military organization composed of both professional and nonprofessional warriors
    4. a military organization composed of nonprofessional warriors

22. Is feuding present?
    1. absent
    2. feuding with compensation
    3. feuding without compensation

23. If there is more than one political community within the culture, how frequently do they war with each other?
    1. continually
    2. frequently
    3. infrequently
    4. never

24. For what reasons does the military organization go to war?
    1. subjugation and tribute
    2. land
    3. plunder
    4. trophies and honors
    5. revenge
    6. defense

25. In what types of supernatural beings do the people believe?
    1. a high god
    2. superior gods
    3. ancestral spirits
    4. nonhuman spirits

26. What types of religious practitioners are present?
    1. absent
    2. shamans
    3. priests

27. What types of magic are practiced?
    1. homeopathic magic
    2. contagious magic

28. Is sorcery practiced?
    1. no
    2. yes

29. How long is the post-partum sex taboo?
    1. absent
    2. short
    3. long

30. What types of games are played?
    1. games absent
    2. physical skill
    3. physical skill and strategy
    4. physical skill and chance
    5. physical skill, strategy, and chance
    6. strategy
    7. strategy and chance
    8. chance

31. What types of initiation rites are present?
    1. initiation rites absent
    2. male initiation rites, step ————
    3. female initiation rites, step ————

32. What types of graphic art are present?
    1. abstract
    2. representational–expressionistic
    3. representational–naturalistic

Glossary

ABSTRACT ART: Graphic art which depends upon formal elements, such as lines, triangles, diamonds, squares, and circles, with the pattern formed from these elements showing such properties as symmetry, repetition, balance, and rhythm.

AFFINAL: Relationship by marriage.

AGRICULTURE: The technology of farming or raising crops with the use of a plow and draft animal.

AMBILINEAGE: A descent group whose membership is based upon a rule of ambilineal descent. Also called RAMAGE.

AMBILINEAL DESCENT: A cultural principle which filiates an individual through either his father or mother to a descent group that consists of only some of his kinsmen.

AMBILOCAL: This form of marital residence pertains to the frequency of both patrilocal and matrilocal residence in a local group or in the culture as a whole. Ambilocal residence occurs if neither patrilocal nor matrilocal residence exceeds the other in actual frequency by a ratio of greater than two to one. Also called BILOCAL.

ANCESTRAL SPIRIT: A supernatural being who is a spirit of a dead person and who plays some role in the affairs of his living relatives.

ANIMAL HUSBANDRY: The practice of breeding and raising domesticated animals.

ANIMISM: Belief in supernatural beings.

AVUNCULOCAL: Marital residence in which the newly wed couple lives with or near a maternal uncle of the groom; that is, the couple joins the household of the husband's mother's brother.

BALANCED RECIPROCITY: Direct exchange in which goods and services of commensurate worth are traded within a finite period.

BOREAL FORESTS: Forests, consisting primarily of conifers, which are characterized by cold, swampy tracts, in which the temperature is usually below 50° Fahrenheit throughout the year and rainfall is slight.

CHANCE, GAME OF: A game in which the outcome is determined by guesses or by some uncontrolled artifact such as a die or a wheel.

CHIEF: A formal political leader with limited power.

CITIES: *See* TOWNS or CITIES.

CLAN: A descent group composed of two or more lineages. Clans are non-localized, they are named, and they are based upon the same rule of descent as the lineages which compose them.

COMMONLOCAL: Marital residence in which the newly wed couple establishes their household in the same local group in which the parental homes of both the man and the woman are located.

COMMUNITY: The maximal group of persons who normally reside together in face-to-face association. When a local group becomes so large that each adult member does not know every other member of the local group, it ceases to be a community.

CONSANGUINEAL: Descended from a common ancestor.

CONTAGIOUS MAGIC: Based on the "law of contact or contagion"; that is, the principle of thought that things which have once been in contact with each other continue to act on each other at a distance after the physical contact has been severed. The practitioner of this type of magic infers that whatever he does to a material object will affect equally the person with whom the object was once in contact.

CONTROLLED COMPARISON: A technique used to demonstrate that factors or culture traits not stated in the hypothesis are not influencing the culture trait which the anthropologist wishes to explain. The technique requires that two highly similar cultures be compared simultaneously.

CROSS-COUSIN: An individual's mother's brother's child or his father's sister's child. Cross cousins are the children of a brother and a sister; that is, the children of opposite sex siblings.

CROSS-COUSIN MARRIAGE: The marriage of a man to either his mother's brother's daughter or to his father's sister's daughter.

CROSS-CULTURAL SURVEY: A research technique which tests hypotheses by comparing simultaneously information from a large number of cultures. Research reports emanating from this method are known as cross-cultural studies.

CROW KINSHIP TERMINOLOGY: Parallel cousins are referred to by the same terms used to refer to brother and sister; father's sister's son is referred to by the term used to refer to father, and father's sister's daughter is referred to by the term used to refer to father's sister; mother's brother's son is referred to as son or brother's son, and mother's brother's daughter is referred to as daughter or brother's daughter.

CULTURE: The way of life of a particular group of people. Culture includes everything that a group of people thinks, and says, and does, and makes.

CULTURE, A: A particular group of people who share the same way of life. The criterion for distinguishing one group of people from another is language. If two groups of people speak different languages, they are different cultures.

CULTURE TRAIT: Although it has been defined as the smallest identifiable unit in a given culture, the term in actual practice is applied to any aspect of a people's way of life.

DESCENT: A cultural principle whereby an individual is socially allocated to a specific group of consanguineal kinsmen.

DESCENT GROUP: A group of consanguineal kinsmen, membership in which is determined by a rule of descent. Descent groups are multigenerational, ancestor-oriented, and include in their membership only descendants of the ancestor.

DESERTS: Dry lands which are characterized by an annual rainfall of less than ten inches.

DICTATOR: An informal political leader with absolute power.

DIFFUSION: The geographic spread of culture traits. It can occur through the acceptance of culture traits from one culture by the members of another culture, or it can occur through the migration or dispersion of local groups belonging to one culture.

DISPERSED HOMESTEADS: Settlement pattern in which the members of the culture reside in permanent homesteads with fields between the homesteads. Homesteads may be from several hundred feet to several hundred yards from each other.

DISTRICT: A territorial unit within a political community which is composed of local groups.

DOUBLE DESCENT: Not a rule of descent per se, but a designation used by anthropologists for a culture which has both patrilineages and matrilineages (and hence both patrilineal and matrilineal descent are present).

EGO: The particular individual from which the relationships between kinsmen (including affinals) are reckoned. This technical term is often found on kinship diagrams.

ENDOGAMY: The practice of marrying a member of one's descent group. It is marriage within either a lineage, clan, or phratry.

ENVIRONMENTAL POSSIBILISM: That point of view which looks upon the physical environment as providing both opportunities and limitations for the way of life of a people living in that environment.

ESKIMO KINSHIP TERMINOLOGY: Cousins are referred to by a distinctive term which is different from the terms used to refer to brother and sister.

ETHNOGRAPHER: An anthropologist who conducts research on the culture of a particular people and who writes a descriptive account of their culture.

ETHNOGRAPHIC PRESENT: The period between the time when Europeans first discovered and observed a culture and the time when the culture's political communities were absorbed into a conquering nation.

ETHNOGRAPHY: A descriptive account of a people's culture. Usually an ethnography describes the culture of a particular social group within the culture.

EXOGAMY: The practice of marrying an individual who is not a member of one's descent group. It is marriage outside either a lineage, clan, or phratry. (Note: It is possible to have lineage exogamy and clan endogamy or to have lineage and clan exogamy and phratry endogamy.)

EXTENDED FAMILY HOUSEHOLD: A domestic group consisting of three (or possibly more) generations of related individuals, including one or more marital groups in each of two adjacent generations.

EXTERNAL WAR: Warfare between culturally different political communities; that is, political communities which are not within the same culture.

FEMALE HEADED HOUSEHOLD: *See* MOTHER-CHILD HOUSEHOLD.

FEUDING: Armed combat within a political community, in which, if a homicide occurs, the kin of the deceased take revenge through killing the offender or a close relative of his.

FEUDING WITH COMPENSATION: Feuding which occurs if the relatives of the deceased sometimes accept compensation in lieu of blood revenge.

FEUDING WITHOUT COMPENSATION: Feuding which occurs if the relatives of the deceased are expected to take revenge through killing the offender or any close relative of his. The possibility of paying compensation does not exist.

FILIATION: Allocation of an individual, through either his father or his mother, to a descent group. (The term may be used more generally to refer to the basis of membership in other than descent groups.)

FRATERNAL JOINT FAMILY HOUSEHOLD: A domestic group composed of two or more brothers, their wives, and their children.

FRATERNAL POLYANDRY: The marriage of one woman to two or more brothers at one time.

FULL-TIME SPECIALISTS: Specialists who devote nearly all of their working time to their specialized task.

GAME: An activity which is characterized by organized play, competition, two or more sides, criteria for determining the winner, and agreed-upon rules.

GENERAL POLYGYNY: This type of polygyny exists if the percentage of polygynous marital groups in a culture ranges between 20 and 100 percent of all marital groups.

GENERALIZED RECIPROCITY: Exchange in which goods and services flow predominantly one-way, with appreciation and respect flowing from the recipient.

GRAPHIC ART: Two-dimensional art which includes painting, drawing, tattooing, and embroidering.

GRASSLANDS: Savannas, prairies, and steepes are classified as grasslands. Grasslands are characterized by rich subsoil, covered with grasses.

GROUP MARRIAGE: The marriage of two or more men to two or more women at one time.

HAMLETS OR COMPACT VILLAGES: Settlement pattern in which the members of a culture reside in permanent homesteads or houses which are close to each other. The population of a hamlet or compact village is not more than 5,000 persons. In some cultures there are compact villages with outlying satellite hamlets.

HAWAIIAN KINSHIP TERMINOLOGY: All male cousins are referred to by the same term which an individual uses to refer to his brother and all female cousins are referred to by the same term which he uses to refer to his sister.

HEADMAN: An informal political leader with limited power.

HETEROGENEOUS POLITICAL COMMUNITY: The local groups composing the political community are from two or more cultures.

HIERARCHICAL LEVEL: An administrative level within a political community. Local groups constitute one level; if local groups are organized into districts this is another level; if districts are organized into provinces this is a third level.

HIGH GOD: A supernatural being who created the universe and/or is the ultimate governor of the universe.

HOMEOPATHIC MAGIC: Based on the "law of similarity"; that is, the principle of thought that like produces like, or that an effect resembles its cause. The practitioner of this type of magic infers that he can produce any effect he desires merely by imitating it.

HOMOGENEOUS POLITICAL COMMUNITY: The local groups composing the political community share the same culture.

HORTICULTURE: The technology of farming or raising crops with the use of hand tools, such as a digging stick or hoe.

HOUSEHOLD: A group of people living together who form a domestic unit. Usually the group occupies a physical structure with walls and a roof which can be described as a house or homestead.

HUNTING AND GATHERING: Includes fishing. Consists of techniques of obtaining natural foodstuffs—animal and vegetable—from the environment.

HYPOTHESIS: A statement of a precise relationship between that which is to be explained and that which is to do the explaining. The relationship is a linkage between two culture traits or two concepts which the anthropologist wishes to test in order to determine the validity of the relationship.

INFORMANT: The individual from whom an anthropologist obtains his information about the way of life of that individual's culture.

INITIATION RITES: Ceremonies, supervised in part by the adults of a culture, which are mandatory for all adolescents of one sex only. If the ceremony is mandatory for all boys, it is a "male initiation rite"; if it is mandatory for all girls, it is a "female initiation rite."

INTERNAL WAR: Warfare between political communities within the same culture.

IROQUOIS KINSHIP TERMINOLOGY: Parallel cousins are referred to by the same terms used to refer to brother and sister, while cross-cousins are referred to by a different term.

KINDRED: An ego-oriented aggregate of kinsmen. A kindred is an aggregate rather than a social group because its membership is composed of individuals who define their respective membership in the aggregate in terms of their relationship to a particular individual.

KINDREDS, AS CATEGORIES OF KIN: An aggregate of kinsmen which consists of all recognized relatives of a particular individual. Such kindreds have a generic name or label.

KINDREDS, AS QUASIGROUPS: An aggregate of kinsmen which consists of those relatives of an individual who have identical rights and obligations with regard to the individual. Such kindreds need not be named, but probably are.

KING: A formal political leader with absolute power.

KINSHIP TERMINOLOGY: The terms used to refer to relatives, either consanguineal or affinal.

LAW: A "case" is legal (that is, law exists) if three elements are present: official authority, privileged force, and regularity.

LAW OF PRIVATE DELICTS: The settlement of a legal case by means of a restitutive sanction.

LAW OF PUBLIC DELICTS: The settlement of a legal case by means of a penal sanction.

LIMITED POLYGYNY: This type of polygyny exists if the percentage of polygynous marital groups in a culture ranges between one and 19 percent of all marital groups.

LINEAGE: Either a patrilineage or a matrilineage.

LINKAGE: A presumed relationship between two culture traits.

LOCAL GROUP: A spatially distinguishable aggregate of people. It may be as small as a single family or as large as a city.

MAGIC, THE PRACTICE OF: Involves three elements: the practitioner, the practical aim or end to be achieved, and the magical formula itself.

MAGICAL FORMULA: The traditional procedures followed by a practitioner (of magic) in carrying out his aims. The formula usually consists of three aspects: the things used—the instruments or medicines; the things done—the rite; and, the things spoken—the spell.

MARITAL GROUP: The group formed when individual men and women enter into one or more marital unions. Marital groups can be either monogamous, polygynous, or polyandrous.

MARITAL RESIDENCE: The location where a couple lives.

MARITAL RESIDENCE RULE: An explicit cultural rule which states where a couple should live.

MARRIAGE: A sexual relationship between a man and a woman who share a common residence. Also called MARITAL UNION.

MARKET EXCHANGE: The exchange of goods and services according to the law of supply and demand.

MATRILATERAL CROSS-COUSIN: A individual's mother's brother's child.

MATRILATERAL CROSS-COUSIN MARRIAGE: A marriage between a man and his mother's brother's daughter.

MATRILINEAGE: A descent group whose membership is based upon a rule of matrilineal descent.

MATRILINEAL DESCENT: A cultural principle which automatically filiates a child at birth through his mother to a descent group that consists of all kinsmen who are related to him through his female ancestors.

MATRILOCAL: Marital residence in which the groom leaves his parental home and lives with his bride, either in the house of her parents or in a dwelling nearby; that is, he joins the household of his wife's parents.

MATRI-PATRILOCAL: Marital residence in which there is an initial period, usually for a year or until the birth of the first child, of matrilocal residence followed by permanent patrilocal residence.

MAXIMAL TERRITORIAL UNIT: An alternate term for political community.

MEDITERRANEAN SCRUB FORESTS: Scrub forests characterized by broadleaf evergreens and oaks, with mild, rainy winters and hot, dry summers prevailing.

MILITARY ORGANIZATION: A particular type of social organization which engages in armed combat with other similar organizations in order to obtain certain goals.

MOIETY: One of two clans or two phratries. A culture has moieties if it has only two clans or two phratries, and every individual is a member of one or the other.

MONEY, GENERAL PURPOSE: Money which serves all three of the following functions: a medium of exchange, a standard of value, and a means of discharging obligations.

MONEY, LIMITED PURPOSE: Money which serves only one or two of the following functions: a medium of exchange, a standard of value, and a means of discharging obligations.

MONOGAMY: The marriage of one man to one woman.

MONOTHEISM: Belief in one god. If a high god is present, but superior gods are not, the religious belief system can be classified as monotheistic.

MOTHER-CHILD HOUSEHOLD: A domestic group composed of a woman, who is either unmarried, widowed, separated, or divorced, and her children, and sometimes her grandchildren. Also called FEMALE HEADED HOUSEHOLD.

MOUNTAINS: A land mass which rises conspicuously above the surrounding region. All seven of the other types of physical environments described in the text may be found on mountains if they are located near the equator.

MULTILINEAL DESCENT: A cultural principle which automatically filiates a child at birth through his father and his mother (and through his four grandparents, and through his eight great grandparents, and so on) to every descent group founded by one of his ancestors.

NEOLOCAL: Marital residence in which the couple establishes a household independent of the location of the parental home of either partner. Specifically this means that they establish their household in a local group other than the local group or groups where their parental homes are located.

NOMADIC: Settlement pattern in which the members of the culture are grouped into small bands which shift from one section of their territory to another throughout the year.

NONHUMAN SPIRIT: A supernatural being who controls a particular individual or place. He may be a guardian spirit, an animal ancestor, or an animal-like creature who has both human and animal attributes.

NUCLEAR FAMILY HOUSEHOLD, INDEPENDENT: A domestic group consisting of a married couple and their children who occupy a dwelling which is not part of any other household.

OEDIPUS COMPLEX: A key term in psychoanalytic theory which refers to the sexual attraction of a boy for his mother, which results in feelings of rivalry and hostility towards his father.

OMAHA KINSHIP TERMINOLOGY: Parallel cousins are referred to by the same terms used to refer to brother and sister; father's sister's son is referred to by the term used to refer to son or sister's son, and father's sister's daughter is referred to by the term used to refer to daughter or sister's daughter; mother's brother's son is referred to as mother's brother and mother's brother's daughter is referred to as mother.

PARALLEL COUSIN: An individual's father's brother's child or his mother's sister's child. Parallel cousins are the children of two brothers or two sisters; that is, the children of same sex siblings.

PARALLEL COUSIN MARRIAGE: The marriage of a man to his father's brother's daughter.

PART-TIME SPECIALISTS: Specialists who devote only a part of their time, either daily or seasonally, to their specialized task.

PATRILATERAL CROSS-COUSIN: An individual's father's sister's child.

PATRILATERAL CROSS-COUSIN MARRIAGE: A marriage between a man and his father's sister's daughter.

PATRILINEAGE: A descent group whose membership is based upon a rule of patrilineal descent.

PATRILINEAL DESCENT: A cultural principle which automatically filiates a child at birth through his father to a descent group that consists of all kinsmen who are related to him through his male ancestors.

PATRILOCAL: Marital residence in which the bride leaves her parental home and lives with her husband, either in the house of his parents or in a dwelling nearby; that is, she joins the household of her husband's parents.

PENAL SANCTION: A punishment inflicted upon an individual who is responsible for violating a rule of conduct.

PHRATRY: A descent group composed of two or more clans. Like clans, phratries are nonlocalized, they are named, and they are based upon the same rule of descent as the clans which compose them.

PHYSICAL SKILL, GAME OF: A game in which the outcome is determined by the players' motor activities.

PLASTIC ART: Three-dimensional art which includes sculpture and ceramics.

POLAR LANDS: Tundra, polar deserts, and permanent ice caps are classified as polar lands. Polar lands are characterized by little snowfall and no forests except for scrub vegetation and dwarf trees.

POLITICAL COMMUNITY: A group of people whose membership is defined in terms of occupancy of a common territory and who have an official with the special function of announcing group decisions—a function exercised at least once a year.

POLITICAL LEADER: The leader, official, or head of a political community.

POLITICAL SYSTEM: The organization of hierarchical levels within a political community.

POLYANDRY: The marriage of one woman to two or more men at one time.

POLYGAMOUS FAMILY HOUSEHOLD, INDEPENDENT: A domestic group consisting of either a polygynous or a polyandrous marital group and its children who occupy a dwelling which is not part of any other household.

POLYGAMY: A term which refers to either polygyny or polyandry.

POLYGYNY: The marriage of one man to two or more women at one time.

POLYTHEISM: Belief in more than one god. If superior gods are present, with or without a high god being present, the religious belief system can be classified as polytheistic.

POPULATION DENSITY: The number of persons per square mile. The formula for computing is as follows:

$$\text{Population Density} = \frac{\text{Population Size}}{\text{Square Miles}}$$

POST-PARTUM SEX TABOO: A rule which prohibits a woman from having sexual intercourse with her husband, or any man, after she has given birth to a child. The post-partum sex taboo is considered "long" if it is observed for twelve months or more; it is considered "short" if it is observed for less than twelve months.

PRIEST: A religious practitioner who devotes nearly all of his time to serving as an intermediary, usually for his local group or political community. He is regarded as a full-time specialist.

PROVINCE: A territorial unit within a political community which is composed of districts.

RAMAGE: *See* AMBILINEAGE.

RECIPROCITY: The exchange of goods and services between units of the same kind, such as individuals, households, kinship groups, or local groups. *See also* BALANCED RECIPROCITY and GENERALIZED RECIPROCITY.

REDISTRIBUTION: The systematic movement of goods and services toward an administrative center and their reallocation by the authorities.

RELIGIOUS PRACTITIONERS: Intermediaries between men and supernatural beings.

REPRESENTATIONAL-EXPRESSIONISTIC ART: Graphic art which depicts people, animals, or natural phenomena, but the treatment of the figures is exaggerated.

REPRESENTATIONAL-NATURALISTIC ART: Graphic art which depicts people, animals, or natural phenomena in a realistic manner.

RESTITUTIVE SANCTION: A requirement that one individual (the defendant) must make payment to the other individual (the plaintiff) in a dispute.

RITES OF INTENSIFICATION: Ceremonies or rituals which express group sentiments and beliefs and which are performed in the presence of most members of the local group.

RITES OF PASSAGE: Ceremonies signifying death and rebirth—the end of one stage of life and the beginning of another. They can be divided into three consecutive major phases: separation, transition, and incorporation. Rites of passage often occur at birth, initiation, marriage, and death.

SEMINOMADIC: Settlement pattern in which the members of the culture spend part of the year in permanent settlements and the remainder of the year migrating as bands.

SHAMAN: A religious practitioner who devotes part of his time to serving as an intermediary, usually for individuals. He is regarded as a part-time specialist.

SHIFTING CULTIVATION: A type of horticulture in which fields are allowed to return to fallow, either bush or jungle. Shifting cultivation is often found in conjunction with slash-and-burn agriculture.

SLASH-AND-BURN AGRICULTURE: A type of horticulture in which the vegetation removed from the land is heaped and burned, and the ash used to fertilize the soil. Slash-and-burn agriculture is often found in conjunction with shifting cultivation.

SORCERY: The use of magic, supernatural beings, or other supernatural powers to deliberately attempt to harm or destroy another person. The individual who practices sorcery is known as a sorcerer.

SPECIALISTS: Members of a culture who perform a task which is not performed by most members of that culture. The products of this task, or the performance of this task itself, may be sold or traded to other members of the culture for goods and services.

STATE: A political community headed by a king or dictator.

STEM FAMILY HOUSEHOLD: A small extended family household consisting of three generations of related individuals, including only one marital group in each of two adjacent generations.

STRATEGY, GAME OF: A game in which the outcome is determined by rational choices among possible courses of action.

SUBSISTENCE TECHNOLOGY: An activity which people perform to exploit their physical environment in order to gain a livelihood.

SUDANESE KINSHIP TERMINOLOGY: Each category of cousin is referred to by a distinct term.

SUPERIOR GOD: A supernatural being who controls all phases of one or more, but not all, human activities.

SUPERNATURAL BEINGS: Beings or spirits which belong to the realm of the supernatural. They are believed to be real (by members of the culture); they have personal identities, and often they have names.

TEMPERATE FORESTS: Forests which are characterized by broadleaf and coniferous trees that obtain their growth from plentiful rain.

TOWNS OR CITIES: Settlement pattern in which the members of a culture reside in permanent homesteads or houses which are close to each other. The population of a town or city is over 5,000 persons. In some cultures there are cities with outlying satellite towns.

TROPICAL FORESTS: Both rain forests and semideciduous forests are classified as tropical forests. Rain forests have heavy daily rainfall which results in dense vegetation. Semideciduous forests have a dry season in which many trees lose their leaves.

TROUBLE CASES: Conflicts or disputes between individual members of the same or of different local groups which create ruptures in intra-political community relationships.

UNRESTRICTED DESCENT GROUP: A descent group whose membership is based upon a rule of multilineal descent.

UXORILOCAL: Marital residence in which the couple establishes their household in a local group in which the woman's parental home is located, but not the man's parental home.

VILLAGES, COMPACT: *See* HAMLETS OR COMPACT VILLAGES.

VIRILOCAL: Marital residence in which the couple establishes their household in a local group in which the man's parental home is located, but not the woman's parental home.

WAR, CAUSES OF: The causes of war—that is, the reasons that military organizations go to war—include subjugation and tribute, land, plunder, trophies and honors, revenge, and defense.

WARFARE: Armed combat between political communities. The frequency of warfare can be classified as either "continual," "frequent," "infrequent," or "never." *See also* EXTERNAL WAR and INTERNAL WAR.

WARRIORS, NONPROFESSIONAL: Military personnel who have not had intensive training in the art of war.

WARRIORS, PROFESSIONAL: Military personnel who devote a substantial part of their time during their early adulthood to intensive training, which may involve not only practice in the use of weapons but also practice in performing maneuvers. They may be members of age-grades, military societies, or standing armies.

WITCHCRAFT: Used synonymously with the term SORCERY in this book.

References

Adams, Richard N., 1960, "An Inquiry into the Nature of the Family," in *Essays in the Science of Culture*, ed. G. E. Dole and R. L. Carneiro. New York: Thomas Y. Crowell Company, pp. 30–49.

Appell, G. N., 1967, "Observational Procedures for Identifying Kindreds: Social Isolates among the Rungus of Borneo," *Southwestern Journal of Anthropology* 23:192–207.

Barry, Herbert, III, 1957, "Relationships between Child Training and the Pictorial Arts," *The Journal of Abnormal and Social Psychology* 54:380–383.

Beals, Alan R. (with George and Louise Spindler), 1967, *Culture in Process*. New York: Holt, Rinehart and Winston, Inc.

Befu, Harumi, and Leonard Plotnicov, 1962, "Types of Corporate Unilineal Descent Groups," *American Anthropologist* 64:313–327.

Boas, Franz, 1955, *Primitive Art*. New York: Dover Publications, Inc. Originally published 1927.

Bohannan, Paul, 1963, *Social Anthropology*. New York: Holt, Rinehart and Winston, Inc.

Brown, Judith, 1963, "A Cross-Cultural Study of Female Initiation Rites," *American Anthropologist* 65:837–853.

Buchler, Ira R., and Henry A. Selby, 1968, *Kinship and Social Organization: An Introduction to Theory and Method*. New York: The Macmillan Company.

Campbell, Donald T., and Robert A. LeVine, 1961, "A Proposal for Cooperative Cross-Cultural Research on Ethnocentrism," *Journal of Conflict Resolution* 5:82–108.

Chagnon, Napoleon A., 1968, *Yąnomamö: The Fierce People*. New York: Holt, Rinehart and Winston, Inc.

Chapple, Eliot, and C. S. Coon, 1942, *Principles of Anthropology*. New York: Holt, Rinehart and Winston, Inc.

Firth, Raymond, 1958, *Human Types: An Introduction to Social Anthropology.* New York: Mentor Book.

Fischer, John L., 1961, "Art Styles as Cultural Cognitive Maps," *American Anthropologist* 63:79–93.

Fortes, Meyer and E. E. Evans-Pritchard, 1940, "Introduction," *African Political Systems*, ed. Fortes and Evans-Pritchard. London: Oxford University Press, pp. 1–23.

Fox, Robin, 1967, *Kinship and Marriage.* Baltimore: Penguin Books, Inc.

Frazer, James G., 1911, *The Golden Bough: A Study in Magic and Religion,* Vol. 1. London: Macmillan & Co., Ltd.

Fried, Morton H., 1967, *The Evolution of Political Society: An Essay in Political Anthropology.* New York: Random House, Inc.

Gamst, Frederick C., 1969, *The Qemant: A Pagan-Hebraic Peasantry of Ethiopia.* New York: Holt, Rinehart and Winston, Inc.

Geertz, Clifford, 1957, "Ritual and Social Change: A Javanese Example," *American Anthropologist* 59:32–54.

Goodenough, Ward H., 1970, *Description and Comparison in Cultural Anthropology.* Chicago: Aldine Publishing Company.

Gough, Kathleen, 1959, "The Nayars and the Definition of Marriage," *The Journal of the Royal Anthropological Institute of Great Britain and Ireland* 89:23–34.

Hays, H. R., 1958, *From Ape to Angel: An Informal History of Social Anthropology.* New York: Capricorn Books.

Herskovits, Melville J., 1948, *Man and His Works: The Science of Cultural Anthropology.* New York: Alfred A. Knopf.

Hoebel, E. Adamson, 1954, *The Law of Primitive Man: A Study in Comparative Legal Dynamics.* Cambridge: Harvard University Press.

Homans, George C., and David M. Schneider, 1955, *Marriage, Authority, and Final Causes: A Study of Unilateral Cross-Cousin Marriage.* New York: The Free Press.

Honigmann, John J., 1959, *The World of Man.* New York: Harper & Row, Publishers.

Leach, Edward R., 1961, *Pul Eliya: A Village in Ceylon.* Cambridge: Cambridge University Press.

Lessa, William A., and Evon Z. Vogt, 1958, *Reader in Comparative Religion: An Anthropological Approach.* Evanston, Ill.: Row, Peterson & Company.

Lévi-Strauss, Claude, 1969, *The Elementary Structures of Kinship* (Les Structures élémentaires de la parenté), trans. of revised ed. by J. H. Bell, J. R. von Sturmer, R. Needham. Boston: Beacon Press. Originally published 1949.

Linton, Ralph, 1936, *The Study of Man: An Introduction.* New York: Appleton-Century-Crofts.

Malinowski, Bronislaw, 1930, "Parenthood—The Basis of Social Structure," in *The New Generation*, ed. V. F. Calverton and S. D. Schmalhausen. New York: The Citadel Press, pp. 113–168.

Mandelbaum, David G., 1963, "A Design for an Anthropology Curriculum," in

The Teaching of Anthropology, ed. D. G. Mandelbaum, G. W. Lasker, and E. M. Albert. American Anthropological Association Memoir 94: 49–64.

———, Gabriel W. Lasker, and Ethel M. Albert, eds., 1963, *The Teaching of Anthropology*. American Anthropological Association Memoir 94.

Mead, Margaret, 1964, "Warfare Is Only an Invention—Not a Biological Necessity," in *War: Studies from Psychology, Sociology, Anthropology*, ed. L. Bramson and G. Goethals. New York: Basic Books, Inc., pp. 269–274.

Mitchell, William E., 1963, "Theoretical Problems in the Concept of Kindred," *American Anthropologist* 65:343–354.

Morgan, Lewis H., 1871, *Systems of Consanquinity and Affinity of the Human Family*. Washington, D.C.: Smithsonian Institution Contributions to Knowledge.

———, 1962, *League of the Iroquois*. New York: Corinth Books. Originally published 1851.

Murdock, George P., 1949, *Social Structure*. New York: The Macmillan Company.

———, 1957, "World Ethnographic Sample," *American Anthropologist* 59: 664–687.

———, 1967, "Ethnographic Atlas: A Summary," *Ethnology* 6:109–236.

———, et al., 1961, *Outline of Cultural Materials*. New Haven: Human Relations Area Files Press.

Naroll, Raoul, 1956, "A Preliminary Index of Social Development," *American Anthropologist* 58:687–715.

———, 1964, "On Ethnic Unit Classification," *Current Anthropology* 5:283–312.

———, 1966, "Does Military Deterrence Deter?" *Trans-action* 3(2):14–20.

———, 1968, "Some Thoughts on Comparative Method in Cultural Anthropology," in *Methodology in Social Research*, ed. H. M. and A. B. Blalock. New York: McGraw-Hill, Inc., pp. 236–277.

Needham, Rodney, 1960, *Structure and Sentiment: A Test Case in Social Anthropology*. Chicago: The University of Chicago Press.

Otterbein, Keith F., 1963, "Marquesan Polyandry," *Marriage and Family Living* 25:155–159.

———, 1964, "A Comparison of the Land Tenure Systems of the Bahamas, Jamaica, and Barbados," *International Archives of Ethnography* 50: 31–42.

———, 1965a, "Conflict and Communication: The Social Matrix of Obeah," *Kansas Journal of Sociology* 3:112–128.

———, 1965b, "Caribbean Family Organization: A Comparative Analysis," *American Anthropologist* 67:66–79.

———, 1966, *The Andros Islanders: A Study of Family Organization in the Bahamas*. Lawrence: University of Kansas Press.

———, 1968a, "Internal War: A Cross-Cultural Study," *American Anthropologist* 70:277–289.

————, 1968b, "Cross-Cultural Studies of Armed Combat," *Studies in International Conflict,* Research Monograph No. 1, *Buffalo Studies* 4(1):91–109.

————, 1969, "Basic Steps in Conducting a Cross-Cultural Study," *Behavioral Science Notes* 4:221–236.

————, 1970a, *The Evolution of War: A Cross-Cultural Study.* New Haven: Human Relations Area Files Press.

————, 1970b, "The Developmental Cycle of the Andros Household: A Diachronic Analysis," *American Anthropologist* 72:1412–1419.

————, and Charlotte Swanson Otterbein, 1965, "An Eye for an Eye, a Tooth for a Tooth: A Cross-Cultural Study of Feuding," *American Anthropologist* 67:1470–1482.

Polanyi, Karl, 1957, "The Economy as Instituted Process," in *Trade and Market in the Early Empires,* ed. K. Polanyi, C. M. Arensberg, and H. W. Pearson. New York: The Free Press, pp. 243–270.

Pospisil, Leopold, 1958, *Kapauku Papuans and their Law,* Yale University Publications in Anthropology 54.

————, 1963, *The Kapauku Papuans of West New Guinea.* New York: Holt, Rinehart and Winston, Inc.

Radcliffe-Brown, A. R., 1952, *Structure and Function in Primitive Society.* New York: The Free Press.

Redfield, Robert, 1952, "The Primitive World View," *Proceedings of the American Philosophical Society* 96(1):30–36.

Rivers, William H. R., 1924, *Social Organization.* New York: Alfred A. Knopf.

Roberts, John M., and Brian Sutton-Smith, 1962, "Child Training and Game Involvement," *Ethnology* 1:166–185.

————, Malcolm J. Arth, and Robert R. Bush, 1959, "Games in Culture," *American Anthropologist* 61:597–605.

Sahlins, Marshall D., 1964, "Culture and Environment," in *Horizons of Anthropology,* ed. Sol Tax. Chicago: Aldine Publishing Company, pp. 132–147.

————, 1965, "On the Sociology of Primitive Exchange," in *The Relevance of Models for Social Anthropology,* ed. Michael Banton. A. S. A. Monographs 1, London: Tavistock, pp. 139–236.

Schapera, Issac, 1956, *Government and Politics in Tribal Societies.* London: C. A. Watts & Co., Ltd.

Schusky, Ernest L., 1965, *Manual for Kinship Analysis.* New York: Holt, Rinehart and Winston, Inc.

Service, Elman R., 1962, *Primitive Social Organization: An Evolutionary Perspective.* New York: Random House, Inc.

Sipes, Richard G., n.d., "War, Sports and Aggression: An Empirical Test of Two Rival Theories." Unpublished manuscript.

Spiro, Melford E., 1968, "Causes, Functions, and Cross-Cousin Marriage: An Essay in Anthropological Explanation," in *Theory in Anthropology,* ed. Robert A. Manners and David Kaplan. Chicago: Aldine Publishing Company, pp. 105–115.

Stephens, William N., 1962, *The Oedipus Complex: Cross-Cultural Evidence.* New York: The Free Press.

Stocking, George W., Jr., 1966, "Franz Boas and the Culture Concept in Historical Perspective," *American Anthropologist* 68:867–882.

Swanson, Guy E., 1960, *The Birth of the Gods*. Ann Arbor: The University of Michigan Press.

Titiev, Mischa, 1943, "The Influence of Common Residence on the Unilateral Classification of Kindred," *American Anthropologist* 45:511–530.

Tylor, Edward B., 1879, "On the Game of Patolli in Ancient Mexico, and its Probable Asiatic Origin," *The Journal of the Royal Anthropological Institute of Great Britain and Ireland* 13:116–131. (Bobbs-Merrill Reprint A-392)

————, 1888, "On a Method of Investigating the Development of Institutions; Applied to Laws of Marriage and Descent," *The Journal of the Royal Anthropological Institute of Great Britain and Ireland* 18:245–270. (Bobbs-Merrill Reprint A-391)

————, 1958, *Primitive Culture*. New York: Harper Torchbooks. Originally published 1871.

van Gennep, Arnold, 1960, *The Rites of Passage*. Chicago: The University of Chicago Press. Originally published 1909.

van Velzen, H. U. E. Thoden, and W. van Wetering, 1960, "Residence, Power Groups and Intra–societal Aggression," *International Archives of Ethnography* 49:169–200.

Vayda, Andrew P., and Roy A. Rappaport, 1968, "Ecology: Cultural and Non-Cultural," in *Introduction to Cultural Anthropology*, ed. James Clifton. Boston: Houghton Mifflin Company, pp. 476–497.

Whiting, Beatrice B., 1950, *Paiute Sorcery*. Viking Fund Publications in Anthropology 15.

Whiting, John W. M., 1959, "Sorcery, Sin, and the Superego: A Cross-Cultural Study of Some Mechanisms of Social Control," in *Nebraska Symposium on Motivation: 1959*, ed. Marshall R. Jones. Lincoln: University of Nebraska Press, pp. 174–197.

————, 1964, "Effects of Climate on Certain Cultural Practices," in *Explorations in Cultural Anthropology*, ed. Ward H. Goodenough. New York: McGraw-Hill, Inc., pp. 511–544.

————, Richard Kluckhohn, and Albert Anthony, 1958, "The Function of Male Initiation Ceremonies at Puberty," in *Readings in Social Psychology*, 3rd ed., ed. E. E. Maccoby, T. M. Newcomb, and E. L. Hartley. New York: Holt, Rinehart and Winston, Inc., pp. 359–370.

Wright, Quincy, 1942, *A Study of War*, Vol. 1. Chicago: The University of Chicago Press.

Young, Frank W., 1965, *Initiation Ceremonies: A Cross-Cultural Study of Status Dramatization*. Indianapolis: The Bobbs-Merrill Company, Inc.

Name and
Title Index

Adams, R. N., 41
Albert, E. M., vi
Anthony, A., 111, 113, 120
Appell, G. N., 57
Arth, M. J., 114, 116

Barry, H., III, 123
"Basic Steps in Conducting a Cross-Cultural Study," 139
Beals, A. R., 3
Befu, H., 50
Boas, F., 2, 122–123
Bohannan, P., 16, 39, 67
Brown, J., 120
Buchler, I. R., 57
Bush, R. R., 114, 116

Campbell, D. T., 70
Chagnon, N. A., 9, 14, 17, 20–21, 23, 25, 27, 30, 33, 40, 44, 54–55, 61, 65, 72, 77, 80–81, 84, 87–88, 90, 92, 98–99, 102, 106, 110, 113, 117–118, 121, 124–125, 127
Chapple, E., 12, 16, 23, 102
Coon, C. S., 12, 16, 23, 102

Evans-Pritchard, E. E., 76

Firth, R., 105
Fischer, J. L., 123
Fortes, M., 76
Fox, R., 41
Frazer, J. G., 105
Fried, M. H., 80

Gamst, F. C., 9–10, 15, 18, 20, 22–23, 25, 27, 30–31, 33–34, 40–41, 44, 55–56, 58, 61, 65, 72, 74, 77–78, 81, 85, 88, 93, 99–100, 103, 107, 110–111, 114, 121, 125, 127
Geertz, C., 3
Golden Bough, The, 105
Goodenough, W. H., 3, 42, 50
Gough, K., 42

Hays, H. R., 123
Herskovits, M. J., 4

Hoebel, E. A., 79–80
Homans, G. C., 59–60
Honigmann, J. L., 102

Kluckhohn, R., 11, 113, 120

Lasker, G. W., vi
Leach, E. R., 3
League of the Iroquois, 114
Lessa, W. A., 102
LeVine, R. A., 70
Levi-Strauss, C., 59
Linton, R., 5

Malinowski, B., 42
Mandelbaum, D. G., vi
Manual for Kinship Analysis, 65
Mead, M., 82
Mitchell, W. E., 57
Morgan, L. H., 62, 114–116
Murdock, G. P., 5–6, 20, 36–39, 43–45, 48, 50, 62, 66

Naroll, R., 2, 26, 68, 71, 84
Needham, R., 59

Otterbein, C., 86, 139
Otterbein, K., 1, 7, 43, 48, 52–53, 82–84, 86, 89, 91, 105, 131–132, 138–139
Outline of Cultural Materials, 6

Plotnicov, L., 50
Polanyi, K., 27–28
Pospisil, L., 57, 75, 80
Primitive Art, 122
Primitive Culture, 96
Primitive Social Organization: An Evolutionary Perspective, 32
Principles of Anthropology, 12

Qemant: A Pagan-Hebraic Peasantry of Ethiopia, The, 9

Radcliffe-Brown, A. R., 62, 79
Rappaport, R. A., 12
Redfield, R., 95
Rites of Passage, The, 119

Subject Index